By the same authors

Dietrich Fischer, *Preventing War in the Nuclear Age* (Croom Helm, London and Canberra, 1984)

Jan Tinbergen, *Economic Policy: Principles and Design* (North-Holland Publishing Company, Amsterdam, 1956 (Forth Revised Printing, 1967))

Jan Tinbergen, *Production, Income and Welfare: the Search for an Optimal Social Order* (Wheatsheaf Books Ltd, 1985)

Warfare and Welfare

Integrating Security Policy into Socio-Economic Policy

Jan Tinbergen
Professor Emeritus of Development Planning
Erasmus University, Rotterdam

and

Dietrich Fischer
Associate Professor of Computer Science
Pace University and Visiting Fellow
Center of International Studies, Princeton

WHEATSHEAF BOOKS · SUSSEX

ST. MARTIN'S PRESS · NEW YORK

First published in Great Britain in 1987 by
WHEATSHEAF BOOKS LTD
A MEMBER OF THE HARVESTER PRESS PUBLISHING GROUP
Publisher: John Spiers
16 Ship Street, Brighton, Sussex
and in the USA by
ST. MARTIN'S PRESS, INC.
175 Fifth Avenue, New York, NY10010

© Jan Tinbergen and Dietrich Fischer, 1987

British Library Cataloguing in Publication Data
Tinbergen, Jan
  Warfare and welfare.
  1. International organization
  I. Title II. Fischer, Dietrich
  321'.04   JC361
  ISBN 0–7450–0325–7

Library of Congress Cataloging-in-Publication Data

Tinbergen, Jan, 1903–
  Warfare and welfare.

  Bibliography: p.
  Includes index.
  1. Welfare economics. 2. Economic security.
3. National security. 4. International organization.
I. Fischer, Dietrich, 1941–   II. Title.
HB846.T55 1987   361.6'1   87–9625
ISBN 0–312–00957–7

Typeset in Times 11 on 12 point by Photo·graphics, Honiton, Devon

Printed in Great Britain by Biddles Ltd, Guildford and King's Lynn

Till Olof Palme, som med inlevelse och engagemang gav så mycket av sin talang, kunskap och energi för en bättre värld

(To Olof Palme, who with sympathy and commitment gave so much of his talent, knowledge and energy for a better world)

Contents

Foreword

The main objective of this book is to integrate security policy into socio-economic policy, for the world at large. Welfare, the main objective of socio-economic policy, depends so heavily, in a negative way, on warfare that a socio-economic policy that neglects the consequences of war is unrealistic. So security policy has to be integrated into a 'generalised' socio-economic policy.

The authors are convinced that the world can best be managed without using war as a policy instrument. Put another way, they believe that security cannot be entrusted to sovereign national decision-making. Decisions on international conflict settlement should be entrusted to supranational institutions, especially the International Court of Justice.

In this book an attempt is made systematically to integrate into one frame the main elements of socio-economic and security policies in the nuclear age, but in the belief that conventional wars also are a crime against humanity and not a means to be used to solve social problems or to settle international disputes.

The book has been written as a contribution to Peace Year 1986. It is dedicated, in his own language, to Olof Palme, who was murdered on 28 February, 1986. He is one of the citizens of a country which, in our view, showed more understanding for future international problems than any other.

We owe thanks to many others and apologise for not being able to mention them all, or even ranking the few we do quote in our references. Moreover, it is not only to authors of related publications that we are indebted. Our wives made many contributions, by encouraging and advising us; our children and grandchildren symbolise future generations to us.

Dietrich Fischer wishes to acknowledge support from the MacArthur Foundation.

We want to thank Wheatsheaf Books for their interest in our new approach and also their copy-editor and reader and, last but not least, Mrs Suze Kleyngeld for her patience and skill in dovetailing paragraphs, sections and chapters so as to approach the publisher's house-style as much as possible.

Jan Tinbergen
Dietrich Fischer

Part I
The Optimum Structure and Management of World Society

1 Survey of Concepts

1.1 CONCEPTS NEEDED

This chapter sets out the concepts needed to design an integrated socio-economic and security order and its policy, to be discussed in the later chapters of Part I. A traditional socio-economic system, a traditional security and an integrated setup will be discussed. This means that we first examine the economist's position, then the peace researcher's, and finally set out our proposed integration of the two. Another way of expressing this is that, as economists, we internalise into the economic setup the security aspect. Of course, the security side might equally call this the internalisation of the socio-economic aspect into their setup. Either way we want to present an interdisciplinary analysis.

A main distinction we propose to make is that between *qualitative* and *quantitative concepts*. Qualitative characterisation of the concepts always constitutes the first step. Quantification may follow, but is not always possible; if it is, it is the second step, yielding supplementary information about the range of the phenomenon under discussion. This information opens up opportunities for further research not possible without quantification. Part of scientific development consists of quantifying or measuring something not measured so far. In physics the colour spectrum was first distinguished qualitatively only (red, orange, yellow, etc.) and later quantified as the wavelength of light. Temperature was first understood as something qualitative (hot, warm, etc.) and later measured in degrees. In economics we first speak of rich and poor people then refine that characterisation by measuring incomes.

Similarly a socio-economic order may be characterised by its *aims* either qualitatively or quantitatively. A qualitative identification of a set of aims may be full employment and balance of payments equilibrium. These aims may be quantified by specifying them as at most 3 per cent unemployment and a figure for the total of imports in the widest sense. Quantified aims are also called *targets*. Similarly the means used to attain the aims—for instance, tax rates—when quantified will be called *instruments*. The same terminology will be used in describing the security order.

In this book the socio-economic and security problems will be approached in a qualitative rather than a quantitative way. Partly we are forced to do so for lack of quantitative data. Where quantitative data are available and relevant we shall use them. Where they are not available or relevant some attempt will be made to fill the gaps. But some of the important problems we have to consider are mostly qualitative. In the terminology of the theory of economic policy (Tinbergen, 1956) it is *reforms* rather than year-on-year economic (or security) *policy* that we propose to deal with. In other words, the social (and security) order will be given the main emphasis, illustrated with the instruments to be used. We justify this choice using an example from civil engineering due to Goudriaan: it is more important to build a sufficiently strong bridge (based on static physics) than to study the dynamics of too weak a bridge's collapsing. Our research too is an attempt to find an order of peaceful stability.

This chapter's list of concepts may be compared with the list of *dramatis personae* in front of a play's text or the list of variables preceding an economic model. The order chosen follows the order in which the concepts enter the analysis. As a consequence the structure of this chapter is roughly the same as that of Chapters 2 to 4 inclusive. Some duplication is unavoidable, as Chapters 2 to 4 constitute an elaboration and refinement of the present chapter.

Before starting an ordered treatment of our subject we want to draw the reader's attention to the massive uncertainties it is beset with, largely because of its nature. Some examples may illustrate this. Among western scientists, politicians and military leaders enormous differences of opinion exist about the aims of Soviet leadership. Some hold the view that the occupation of Western Europe is among their aims, others deny this emphatically. Then, among scientists, a wide divergence of opinion exists about the possibilities of finding a technology to protect us against missile attacks. President Reagan's advisors are optimistic about such technological development. Most independent scientists—for instance, those united as 'Concerned Scientists'—are highly sceptical, and call the Strategic Defence Initiative (SDI) 'bizarre' (Rathjens and Ruina, 1985). Equally wide differences of opinion exist about the stability of the balance created by ballistic missile defence (BMD).

Very concrete uncertainties also exist, such as the question of the 'missile gap': for a long time US military leaders maintained that the Soviet Union had many more missiles than the United States. Once spy satellites were available to check the number of missiles, it was found that a gap did exist—but one which favoured the US.

1.2 QUALITATIVE SOCIO-ECONOMIC CONCEPTS: IDEOLOGIES, AIMS AND MEANS

Since a major role in today's economic and security debate is being played by the superpowers (the Soviet Union and the United States—which for reasons of symmetry we shall indicate in this book by SU and US) ideologies are the first concept we encounter. We define an ideology as a theory or an opinion held not by scholars but by politicians and some of the general public, and is more dated than theories discussed by scientists, although the latter are not completely free from ideologies. The main subject covered by an ideology is the impact of a social order on a population's welfare and security.

The two main ideologies used in the world political debate find their origin with Adam Smith (1776) as the father of 'capitalism' and Karl Marx (1867, etc.) of 'communism'. Put this way the ideologies are oversimplified and the extremes of capitalism and communism are inaccurate terms. Even though libraries of literature deal with these issues which the present authors contributed to, we think it appropriate here to restrict ourselves to this over-simplified and inaccurate statement: the argument of this book would not change significantly if we went into more scientific detail at this stage. We do so later. Targeted aims can be summarised as *optimal welfare*. Welfare or human satisfaction indicates the extent to which human needs are satisfied. Human beings are complex creatures with many needs. The details of welfare and its determinants will be discussed in section 2.2.

The socio-economic order created by a nation's authorities (Parliament and government) constitutes, in principle, the means to optimise the population's welfare. By 'order' we mean a set of institutions which all have a number of specific means or instruments. These institutions include traditional and natural groupings such as families, local communities and more consciously designed organisations such as enterprises (production units) up to government authorities at various levels (municipalities, provinces and the central government in Canada or the Netherlands, and similar institutions with other names elsewhere). A particular group of institutions (e.g. schools at various levels) fulfil separate tasks. Public authorities make decisions about a number of community tasks, such as internal law and order, provision of physical and psychical infrastructure, such as means of communication, information and policing, as well as the collection of the taxes and social security contributions needed to implement the authorities' statutory tasks. These concern *collective* or *public goods* whose characteristic is that one individual's use of them does not reduce the possibility for other individuals also to use them. The quantities of these goods needed must be such that the sum of all citizens' marginal utility equals the goods' marginal costs. (The authorities estimate the individuals' marginal utilities.)

A nation's institutions may also include private organisations, from productive units, mentioned before, to consumptive associations of many kinds, sports clubs, arts associations, religious communities, at both the local and international level. In many countries citizens are free to organise themselves in political parties, trade unions and employers' associations, often with superstructures, such as a congress of trade unions, or of employers' federations. In other countries less or little freedom prevails and more of these tasks are considered to be within the government's sphere.

1.3   QUANTITATIVE SOCIO-ECONOMIC CONCEPTS: MODELS, TARGETS AND INSTRUMENTS

As observed, part of the aims and means can be quantified and their interconnections indicated with the help of mathematical relations. In several respects these figures (usually called *variables*) and their mathematical *relations* can be seen as a framework determining the main appearance (German: *Gestalt*) of a nation's economy. Together they are called a model, to underline the simplified nature of such a framework. The variables may be distinguished in four categories (cf. Tinbergen, 1956): data, targets, instruments and other variables. Data are variables whose value is determined outside the socio-economic sphere, for instance scientific development or nature. In this book it is important that variables determined in the security sphere belong in this category.

Models can be used to analyse or to manage an economy—in more detail or more accurately over short periods, or only the main features over long periods. In this book management is chosen as our subject rather than analysis or explanation. This implies that we take as given the data and the targets, and as unknown the instruments and other variables. Important targets for a long-run socio-economic policy are population, production, employment, consumption, investment, income distribution, price levels. This is a minimum list for nations preferring a decentralised policy and leaving many decisions to private employers and markets. Nations with a centralised policy need a large number of targets referring to a considerable number of industrial sectors (in the wide sense of also including primary production (agriculture and mining) and tertiary production (services, from transportation to teaching)).

More features of the models discussed may be taken from economies half-way between complete centralisation and complete decentralisation. Such economies can be found in Western Europe, Japan and some developing countries, whereas the SU and US are more extreme. In such economies stable markets can be left unregulated, but unstable markets are better planned. Examples of the latter are several raw material markets, but possibly also some labour markets. The main cause of the instability of such different types of market are the long lags in the supply relations. A high price for rubber works through an over-supply only after the newly planted trees bear latex. It takes some time to train the increased number of students for a highly skilled type of labour (e.g. a computer programmer). Investment in large buildings and heavy equipment requires planning in order to avoid over- or underinvestment *vis-à -vis* what seems the most desirable rate of growth from various points of view, including environmental considerations. Another cause of market instability is *low elasticities* on both the demand and the supply sides. An aspect to be taken up in more detail in Chapters 5 and 6 is the need to plan for large parts of the world if not for the world as a whole.

The important mathematical relations in socio-economic

models are: *balance equations, production functions* and *demand equations*. Balance equations are important because of the desirability for the economy to develop along a *balanced path*, meaning in many cases the avoidance of over- or underproduction of goods or of skills. Production functions in the widest sense are important since they represent *technological constraints* but also *choices*. Demand equations are important if a maximum of consumer satisfaction is desired.

1.4   SOLUTION OF THE OPTIMUM PROBLEM

We propose to discuss first the concepts used in an exact solution of the optimum order problems. Later we add some remarks on possible approximations. The solution starts by expressing the nation's welfare level in terms of the possible means and instruments to be used. For non-quantified means the relation between welfare and means can only be expressed verbally, or in a table showing qualitative characteristics. The optimum is the maximum of welfare within the frame of the restrictions on the economy. A simple example why restrictions occur is the following. Generally welfare experienced will be higher the more goods are available. Welfare for most people will also be higher the less they have to do onerous work. So at first sight most people will opt for as many goods as possible and as little unpleasant work as possible. But these two options are incompatible, because access to a large quantity of goods requires that a large quantity of unpleasant work be done. This relationship between quantity of goods and quantity of labour—known as a production relationship or *production function*—is one of the restrictions we are facing. The optimum is the point where one more unit of product provides as much satisfaction as the additional labour dissatisfaction. Beyond that point total satisfaction declines.

Other restrictions are to be found in our environment. More production also causes more pollution. Here again a point is reached where the additional pollution provides dissatisfaction equal to the satisfaction derived from the polluting activity.

The education process an individual chooses introduces its own restrictions. Learning more will enable that person to get a job providing more satisfaction—either psychologically or by a higher money income. But a point is reached where more learning is too difficult, depending on the person's capabilities.

Still other restrictions are the balance equations, mentioned before. They express the fact that no more of some input (e.g. energy) can be used than is available. This naturally applies to all inputs. The restrictions will be discussed in more detail in Chapter 3. There are different methods to find a maximum of some variable—welfare, in our case—within a framework of restrictions. In our illustrations for mathematically trained readers we shall choose the method known as 'Lagrange multipliers'. More advanced readers may prefer newer methods. We shall also offer a more advanced method, in some cases. Elsewhere, simpler methods will be used. Sometimes the exact method will be approximated only, instead of being applied strictly. Some applications of the quantitative models described in section 1.3 are based on the assumption that the policy planner knows what values a number of targets have in the optimum, for instance the employment target and the balance of payments discussed in section 1.1.

Some examples of more concrete elaborations of the solutions discussed are shown elsewhere (Tinbergen, 1985). In Chapter 5 of that book a static model is used to find the structure of an economy with I consumers, H producing firms, J private or individual goods and K (part) collective goods. The economy's government estimates the marginal utility of collective goods (which may be part-collective) and collects the taxes to finance their production. Consumers maximise their welfare and producers their profits. The quantity of capital is given; the social order is one of free competition.

In Chapter 14 a dynamic model is used to find an optimal mobile social structure. One good is considered, part of which is consumed, another part invested in physical capital, and a third part in human capital (i.e. education, which transforms each individual's innate quality into a higher quality). Total production depends on capital and on the quality of all I individuals.[1]

1.5　SECURITY: QUALITATIVE AIMS AND MEANS

After discussing the concepts used in a traditional socio-economic setup to find an optimal order and its policy we now consider a traditional polemological setup. The aim may be defined here as *optimal security* with respect to the rest of the world. In the simplest setup only two countries will be considered. This may be interpreted in two ways. One is that the rest of the world is considered as one other nation. The other interpretation—not so far from reality—is to consider only the two superpowers, US and SU. Security has been called an 'underdeveloped concept'. This is illustrated by the fact that some experts (Röling, 1984) consider it to have no less than four dimensions (to be discussed later; see section 2.2), whereas others (Fischer, 1984) see it as one-dimensional. This lack of agreement also appears in the question of whether we consider security as a commodity (a good) or a state of mind of the dimension of welfare. Security refers to the situation of one's nation: its functioning should not be threatened, but, on the contrary, be assured. The feeling of security is narrowly connected with national pride (also called patriotism or nationalism). Most citizens feel happy, when returning from abroad, to be back in their own country. An important aspect of this sense of well-being is the ability to communicate freely with others, who can understand the language spoken. Most people only have one or two languages and they feel lost wherever these languages are not spoken or understood. Another aspect of patriotism is that their education has contributed to the belief that their own nation and its population are better than other nations and their populations. Finally, even if in some respect their country has been shown not to be better—in whatever sense—than some other nation, they may nevertheless feel: 'my country, right or wrong'. All this illustrates the strong emotions generated by nationalism and hence also by the country's security.

The means available to maintain or maximise a country's security consist of various institutions. One considered very important by many, is the country's sovereignty. This implies freedom of determination without recourse to any other nation or institution. Within this freedom, however, treaties with other countries may be concluded. Other institutions making for optimal security may be internal or external political institutions. An internal political institution may be made in matters of trade and development cooperation. An external political institution may be the acceptance of a decision by the International Court of Justice or of another international court. In addition to political institutions military institutions exist and are considered as a means of attaining optimal security. Military institutions are characterised by their human production factors and their arms categories. Broad categories of the latter are conventional and nuclear arms. Another subdivision of great importance is offensive *vs.* defensive weapons.

Galtung (1984) derives defensiveness and offensiveness from the range of the weapons in a system and their impact area, and hence from geographical criteria: if the point of impact is a country's own territory, the system is defensive. Both are designed to serve the own nation's security, but offensive weapons reduce other nations' security, which is not true of defensive arms. Whereas for some types of weaponry defensive arms are well known and numerous, this not (yet) true of rockets. Mines and anti-tank guns can be quite effective, but defence systems against rocket attacks hardly exist. A defensive weapon known to one country, but not to the other, may be dangerous to the latter, however, as explained in section 3.5 in a discussion of the Strategic Defence Initiative.

An institution of decisive importance is a form of cooperation called common security. This means security based on a complete sharing of all technological knowledge about defensive weaponry. With the present distrust between the superpowers' military and political leadership it seems completely illusory. Among scientists it is not illusory. Top scientists prefer international cooperation over nationalism. The threat created by nuclear energy has strengthened scientists' conviction that their traditional attitude is the only guarantee of real security. There seems to be a beginning of understanding between civil servants (Spoor, 1985; Boutwell and Long, 1986).

1.6   SECURITY: QUANTITATIVE TARGETS AND INSTRUMENTS

As in the case of socio-economic policies, details of security policies can be treated in a quantitative way only. Concrete decisions always require figures. That means the setting of targets and the application of instruments. A long-term optimal security order may have zero targets for offensive and low targets for defensive weapons, with the latter only for policing services. Non-military targets in trade may be the absence of import quotas and budgets for financial transfers to countries in difficulties. It is virtually impossible to deal with this subject at present, with the lack of information over long periods.

We consider it more useful to treat a subject linked to quantitative targets and instruments, for a shorter-term discussion as will be presented in Part II of this book. Quantities can be given only after categories have been defined and for readers not familiar with security literature—presumably a substantial number—something may be said about weapon categories and the source of their names. These have their origin in the natural sciences.

Weapons may have a fixed location (mines, anti-aircraft guns) or be mobile. They may move along the surface (tanks, warships) above the surface or below (submarines). The greatest variety is in weapons moving above the surface.

Oldest are *ballistic weapons*, launched from guns and moving along the well-known parabola-like curve, starting at the gun's end and finishing at or near the target. The first ballistic weapons presumably were bullets; early developments consisted of increases in the bullet's size and corresponding increases in the energy used to propel the projectile. In the 1930s the Nazis developed rockets (the V-1 and V-2s), launched in a more complicated way: i.e. with more than one launcher. After World War II some of the German missile engineers were kidnapped by the US and some by the SU, and again size and power were increased. Also, the distance between launching base and target increased. *Strategic missiles* are now able to cross the Atlantic.

The discovery of *nuclear energy* constituted another development. Among the latest developments is the installation on such a missile of more than one vehicle directed at different targets, which required the construction of *multiple independently targetable re-entry vehicles* or MIRVs. Apart from these various developments the accuracy and reliability were improved.

Alongside missiles, *satellites* are used either for peaceful purposes or passive military purposes (e.g. observation). To keep an object such as a satellite in an *orbit*, it has to be launched in a specific direction. A satellite may have orbits in different planes and with different periods. If the plane coincides with that of the earth's equator and the circulation time is 24 hours, the satellite will remain above the same point of the equator (geo-stationary orbit).

The moving forces of ballistic missiles and satellites are the force used for the launching and gravity.

As a defence against ballistic missiles or against observation ('spying') satellites, anti-ballistic (ABM) or anti-satellite (ASAT) missiles may be launched. Both have been tested with varying degrees of success.

Missiles may have auxiliary missiles attached able to change the direction of trajectile. This is not only a characteristic of the much more complicated hardware such as space labs but also for extremely accurate warheads equipped with a terminal guidance system, such as the submarine-launched Trident D-5, now under development in the US.

Finally, delivery vehicles for nuclear weapons include bombers and cruise missiles, which travel close to the earth's surface.

1.7 SECURITY OPTIMUM IS ITS MAXIMUM WITHIN A FRAME OF RESTRICTIONS

Considering security as a collective state of mind reflecting the assumed *probability that now and in the future the functioning of the nation is guaranteed* we shall discuss what the optimum level of security is. As with welfare, the optimum is the maximum level within a framework of restrictions. Before specifying the restrictions the nation is facing, a few remarks on an optimum (and a maximum) are necessary. They represent an *equilibrium*, but a distinction can be made between *stable* and *unstable* *equilibria*. An equilibrium position is the outcome of movements—in our case of the two countries' security position. These movements in the security field are reactions to previous movements of the other country. If the movements converge they lead to a stable equilibrium; if they diverge, the equilibrium is unstable and can only be maintained by external forces. Left to itself the system may engage in an arms race with dangerous implications.

Two forms of instability have been distinguished: *arms race instability* and *crisis instability*. Arms race instability means that the two conflicting sides have an incentive to spend ever larger amounts on weapons. Crisis instability means that in case of a crisis a conflict tends to escalate rapidly, particularly when both sides have an incentive to strike first. The two forms of instability may go together, but they need not.

The restrictions under which security is generated depend to a high degree on the *scenario* we consider. As a consequence of the enormous threats with which we are faced, we shall consider a wide variety of scenarios, in the hope of finding one more attractive than today's. It is characteristic of today's international anarchy that an almost unrestricted sovereignty exists and is even advocated by political leaders. This means the virtual absence of restrictions and the existence of an enormous over-armament, since sovereign nations think that more armaments make for security. In actual fact our security has declined and so has our welfare.

A better scenario is one in which a number of *treaties* have been concluded and are being respected, such as bans on certain types of armaments or on testing new types. The restrictions of the system evidently are the limitations agreed on in the treaties. They may imply a somewhat less dangerous optimum level of security.

In the longer run much better scenarios may become possible, scenarios to be discussed in this book. They introduce the creation increasingly efficient supra-national institutions, whose purpose is an *optimally managed planet*. To achieve it, parts of national sovereignty have to be transferred to a world level.

In the conventional approach (optimal security only) the institutions deal with security, disregarding socio-economic welfare—for instance, an ideal UN Security Council—without considering supra-national institutions in the fields of trade or financial and monetary aims.

1.8 INTEGRATION OF TRADITIONAL SOCIO-ECONOMIC AND SECURITY STRUCTURES AND POLICIES

As announced in the Foreword, the main objective of this book is to integrate the socio-economic and the security search to present an optimal structure of society and the optimal policies characteristic of such a structure. Another way of defining this objective is to call it the internalisation of security policies into socio-economic policies (or, the other way round, the internalisation of socio-economic policies into security policies). This implies not only that the aims and the means of the two have to be combined in an integrated structure and policy, but also that the *cross-impacts* of each component's means on the other component's aims are considered. Because of the increased militarisation of the superpowers, in particular, but also of the rest of the world (including the Third World) these cross-impacts are considerable. The result of this integration means that, in the long run, a considerable contribution to the world's welfare and security can be attained if the mutual suspicion of East and West can be tranformed into a spirit of cooperation.

NOTE

1. On pages 155 and 157 of this chapter some errors have been printed; the correct formulae (14.4), (14.12), (14.13) and (14.14) can be obtained at request from the author.

REFERENCES

Boutwell, J. and F.A. Long (1986), *Weapons in Space*, American Academy of Arts and Sciences, Cambridge, MA.

Fischer, D. (1984). *Preventing War in the Nuclear Age*, London and Canberra, Croom Helm.

Galtung, J. (1984), *There are Alternatives!* Nottingham, Spokesman.

Marx, Karl (1867, 1885, 1893), *Das Kapital*, vols I–III.

Rathjens, G. and Ruina, J. (1985), 'BMD and Strategic Instability', *Daedalus*, Summer 1985, 239–55.

Röling, B.V.A. (1985), 'Bewapening, ontwapening, ontwikkeling en veiligheid' [Armament, disarmament, development and security], in B. Goudzwaard (ed.), *Economie, bewapening en ontwikkeling* [Economics, armament and development], Alphen aan den Rijn, Samson.

Smith, Adam (1776), *The Wealth of Nations*.

Spoor, A. (1985), 'Defensieschild alleen samen met Russen acceptabel' (Defense shield only acceptable together with the Russians), *NRC/Handelsblad*, 11 February 1985, p. 8.

Tinbergen, J. (1956, 4th revised printing 1967), *Economic Policy: Principles and Design*, Amsterdam, North-Holland Publishing Company.

—— (1985), *Production, Income and Welfare*, Brighton, Wheatsheaf Books.

2 Aims: Optimal Welfare-Cum-Security

2.1 WELFARE-CUM-SECURITY AS A GENERALISED CONCEPT

As announced in section 1.8, this chapter deals in more detail with the integration of socio-economic and security optimal orders and their policies into one combined optimal order and its policies. The main reason for this integration is, of course, the disastrous impact a war would have on human welfare. But even in years of peace between the leading countries the resources spent on war preparation are no longer negligible, especially in the SU and the US, and amount to many times the amount spent on development cooperation. So far the only exceptions to this are Japan, Brazil and Mexico, where only 2 per cent or less of GNP is spent on military purposes. Yet this is about twice the amount spent on official development aid. In comparison to the superpowers and the European Community this low military budget makes available to investment, and hence to growth, sizeable amounts, explaining the high rate of growth of the Japanese economy.

Symbolically the integration we are going to study may be said to combine the *problématique* considered by two well-known Independent Commissions of experts with political experience, presided over, respectively, by Willy Brandt and Olof Palme, and known as the Brandt Commission and the Palme Commission. The Brandt Commission reported in 1980 and 1983 under the titles *North–South* and *Common Crisis*; these reports deal with the North–South problem. The Palme Commission reported in 1982 under the title *Common Security*, and deals with the East–West problem.

As a matter of course a combined analysis constitutes an enrichment to all parties concerned. Far better solutions to

North–South problems, including today's most pressing debt problems, would be possible if, simultaneously, a solution—or a half-way solution!—of the East–West problem were implemented. At the same time, some of the tensions in the undeveloped continents would be reduced if more resources were spent on development cooperation, and at least some of the possible reasons for confrontation between the superpowers might be eliminated. The role economists might play in the security debate by integrating it into their field of responsibility would produce additional arguments in favour of a considerable redirection of resources instead of leaving the discussion to military experts alone. If we would only analyse the combined *problématique* as a problem of optimal management of our planet new perspectives would emerge.

The aims the optimal order must set itself may now be formulated as optimal welfare-cum-security or optimal generalised welfare. In this chapter these aims will be considered in more detail.

2.2 WELFARE: ITS COMPONENTS AND DETERMINANTS

A nation's welfare is composed of the welfare of its citizens. Our interpretation of this statement (which is not shared by all economists) is that the nation's welfare is the sum of the welfare of the citizens. This interpretation implies the possibility of measuring an individual's welfare. Welfare may be said to reflect the degree to which each of a number of the individual's needs is considered to be satisfied. Humans are complex beings and have many needs. These can be grouped in various ways. We propose to make a distinction between *individual* and *social* needs. The former depend on the individual's situation in isolation, and the latter on his relation to other individuals. Next, individual needs may be either *material* or *spiritual*. Examples of material individual needs are the need for food, for protection against extremes of climate, or against other environmental forces. This need is satisfied by clothing, dwelling or workplace, and climate. This list can be expanded and each item can be subdivided.

Spiritual needs are those for some degree of freedom, for understanding the environment, the need to perform a task, and so on.

Social needs concern good relations within the family, with colleagues, and friends, etc. up to good relations with certain groups in society, or what might be called the need for a good social climate in which the individual or relatives and friends are living. The word 'relations' reminds us of the importance of the respect each person receives from his or her fellow citizens. In countries where basic needs are satisfied the welfare of each citizen is almost entirely determined by his or her acceptance within the reference group and hardly ever by the absolute level of well-being (cf. Kapteyn, 1982). In countries where basic needs are not fulfilled, the absolute level of satisfaction does of course codetermine the level of welfare.

In this book three models will be presented in order to illustrate the concepts introduced. Readers not interested in the mathematical approach may skip these sections without the risk of not understanding the general argument.

In *Model A* we consider a 'world' consisting of two nations of equal size and level of technology. Their welfare depends on their economic prosperity (measured here by the production of civilian goods) and on their security, which is determined by the quantity and type of a nation's own armaments and those of the other nation. Purely defensive armaments are defined here as those which increase a nation's own security without reducing the security of the other nation. Purely offensive arms are defined as those which reduce the security of the other nation without contributing to the security of the nation acquiring those arms. We shall also consider intermediate types of arms of varying degrees. It is even conceivable to think of 'super-defensive' arms which increase the security of both countries, and 'super-offensive' arms which decrease the security of both. (This model is described in more detail in Fischer, 1984.)

Model A will be solved in two versions: Problem I and Problem II. In Problem I, decisions are taken independently by each nation, whereas in Problem II decisions are taken at the world level, taking into account the welfare of both nations.

Model A considers development over time, in discrete periods. The two nations are assumed to seek to maximise the growth rates of their economies, of both civilian goods and 'security'. A Von Neumann model (a generalised form of the input–output model) is used to describe the quantities of inputs required for production at the beginning of each period, and the outputs produced at the end of each period. The ratio between inputs

Table 2.1

Industries operated by country 1	Inputs from country 1 civ. sec.		Outputs to country 1 civ. sec.		Inputs from country 2 civ. sec.		Outputs to country 2 civ. sec.	
1. civilian	1	0	b	0	0	0	0	0
2. military	1	0	0	c	0	d	0	0

civ. = civilian goods, sec. = national security

and outputs in each sector is equal to the growth factor ($=1 +$ growth rate) of that sector. The goal is to make the smallest of all growth rates as large as possible.

There are two industries in each country, the civilian and the military, and two goods, civilian goods (for both consumption and investment) and 'security'. Both industries use only civilian goods as inputs from the domestic economy, since weapons can neither be consumed nor used to produce other goods or weapons. The required inputs include consumption by workers and their families. For one unit of inputs, the civilian industry produces b units of output (where $b > 1$ for a growing economy). The military industry produces c units of 'security' as domestic output, and uses d units of 'security' as input from the other country. If the arms are purely defensive, $d = 0$. If the arms are purely offensive, $c = 0$. In general, the larger c and the smaller d, the more defensive are the arms produced.

The following coefficients describe the inputs and outputs of the industries operated by country 1, if an industry is operated with 'unit intensity'. If an industry is operated at higher or lower intensity, all coefficients are multiplied by a constant factor greater or less than 1. A symmetric table describes the technology of the industries of country 2.

The policy instruments available to each country are the fraction of each period's civilian outputs it devotes to the civilian and military industries, and the type of armaments it builds.

For Problem II, we have a single table describing the input and output coefficients for the world. The negative externalities of operating the military industry, the reduction of security of the other country, become internalised. The following table describes this situation:

Table 2.2

Industry		World civ.	Inputs sec.	World civ.	Outputs sec.
1.	civilian	1	0	b	0
2.	military	1	d	0	c

Restrictions and optimum conditions will be discussed in section 3.9 and the solutions in section 4.8.

In *Model B* we assume that a nation's welfare ω_i depends on four variables, where $i = 1$ or 2:

y_i the nation's average income
z_i the inequality of income distribution
u_i the rate of unemployment prevailing in that country, and
e_i the state of the environment, where the latter three are
   expressed in terms of income:

$$\omega_i = y_i - z_i - u_i + e_i \qquad (2.2)$$

Now we turn to a third model, *Model C*. We offer it in two versions: Problem I and Problem II. Problem I deals with decisions taken by sovereign nation 1 in a world of two sovereign nations; Problem II with common decisions of these two nations, hence at 'world level'.

The variables for nation i ($i = 1, 2$) are, for both versions:
x_i total production of goods and services
y_i total expenditure on consumption, investment, export surplus, except v_2 (see below)
a_i expenditure on offensive armament
b_i expenditure on defensive armament
v_2 expenditure on goods of special importance to nation 2 and made available by nation 1 only during peace periods.

For version Problem I, $i = 1$ only, but for nation 2 we have
$a_2 = a_2^o$
$b_2 = b_2^o$, i.e. the armament expenditures are considered to be predetermined.

Also in Problem I nation 1 aims at maximising its welfare-cum-security function.

$$\omega_1 = 1n(y_1 - v_2 + 1) + \alpha_{11} 1n(a_1 + 1) - \alpha_1 1n(a_2^o + 1)$$
$$+ \beta_{11} 1n(b_1 + 1) + \beta_{12} 1n(b_2^o + 1) \qquad (2.2 \cdot 1)$$

where α and β are coefficients indicating the impact of the logarithms concerned on welfare of the country considered (reflected by the first index attached to the α or β). The second index refers to the country whose armaments impact the term specifies. Welfare in the traditional sense is represented by the terms in y_1 and security by those in v_2, a_1, b_1 and the given a_2^o and b_2^o. The restrictions which country 1 faces will be discussed in section 3.9 where the optimum conditions will be discussed. This applies also to Problem II for which the aims are to maximise:

$$\begin{aligned}
\Omega = \omega_1 + \omega_2 &= 1n(y_1 - v_2 + 1) + \alpha_{11} 1n(a_1 + 1) \\
&\quad - \alpha_{12} 1n(a_2 + 1) + \beta_{11} 1n(b_1 + 1) + \beta_{12} 1n(b_2 + 1) \quad (2.2 \cdot 2) \\
&\quad + 1n(y_2 + v_2 + 1) - \alpha_{21} 1n(a_1 + 1) + \alpha_{22} 1n(a_2 + 1) \\
&\quad + \beta_{21} 1n(b_1 + 1) + \beta_{22} 1n(b_2 + 1)
\end{aligned}$$

Here Ω is total welfare of both countries. All (Greek) coefficients are positive and the aim function reflects the theory that offensive weapons of the other country affect security negatively, but the other nation's defensive weapons affect security positively. Making available v_2 to country 2 by country 1 constitutes a non-military security instrument. The countries are supposed to have about the same size population.

2.3 SECURITY, OR THE PROBABILITY OF PEACE

Human happiness not only depends on socio-economic welfare as described in the preceding section. In today's world, composed of a number of independent, sovereign nations, some powerful, others with modest or hardly any power, the individual's happiness also depends on his or her nation's security. It is not easy to define the concept of security. Its main elements can be summarised by the probable level of independence or sovereignty of the nation; that is, the probable extent to which the *functioning of its institutions can be determined by the nation's inhabitants*. We also call this the *probability of peace*. This probable level of sovereignty will have a greater impact on the citizens' happiness the more ardent is the country's patriotism or nationalism.

This relatively simple definition of security reflects the role played, in the formulation of this state of mind, by sovereignty and by patriotism. Both these elements contain dubious or irrational aspects. Thus, it is believed that sovereignty means more control over a nation's role; but this is a misconception. A sovereign country's position is also dependent on other sovereign countries' acts. Sometimes it may be better for a country to be party to an alliance with countries that otherwise might act to its detriment.

Patriotism or nationalism may be defined as the belief that one's own country is superior—in whatever sense—to other countries. This cannot, however, be true of all countries. Thus patriotism or nationalism are in part irrational.

Both the misunderstanding of sovereignty and the irrationality of nationalism raise doubts about the 'real' relevance, in terms of human happiness, of security. Security as a mental state can be easily influenced by ideologies, indoctrination and propaganda instead of by real human needs.

So far we have discussed security as a one-dimensional probability of a nation's independent or autonomous functioning in a given period. We shall come back to this when, we discuss the possibilities of measuring security in section 2.5.

Another definition of security is based on the probability of avoiding war and the probability of survival in case of war (Fischer 1984).

Some experts (cf. Röling, 1985) think of a concept of more (in his case four) dimensions: Röling speaks of economic, ideological, enemy and weapon security, where the latter two together are also called military security. Economic security refers to the probability that economic needs can be satisfied, especially the needs for basic commodities (fuel, food). Ideological security depends on whether the nation's ideology is threatened by counter-propaganda in one way or another. Enemy security possibly comes closest to what we discussed under the terms 'sovereignty' and 'patriotism'. Weapon security, in Röling's words (ibid., 158), depends on the nature of the weapons available: insecurity being maximal when these weapons invite a 'first strike' ('use them or lose them').

This brings us close to the basic question of whether security should be defined as a state of mind, comparable to welfare, or as the commodities determining that state of mind. The latter is comparable to defining welfare as the quantities or value of the consumption goods determining welfare. For some purposes (for instance, a simple illustration of the main structure of a social order) the latter approach is appropriate.

2.4   CORRECTION OF PREFERENCES

It is characteristic of socio-economic policy that citizens' preferences are manipulated by their governments while formulating that policy. That means that actual policy is not based on existing preferences but on *corrected preferences*. Important examples are corrections on too short-sighted (myopic) preferences. We know several examples where individuals would later have regretted it if they had stuck to these shortsighted preferences. They will even be pleased that their government stopped them yielding to their own myopia. The clearest example is compulsory schooling, which is now applied almost universally. Other examples are the taxation of unhealthy consumer goods, such as alcoholic beverages or tobacco products, or the prohibition of smoking in public buildings (as in Seattle, Washington). Positive corrections are the making available at low, subsidised, prices, of healthy goods or services: school lunches, less polluting forms of transportation, etc.

Correction of myopic preferences may very well constitute one of the means of a policy aiming at optimal welfare-cum-security. The present policies of the superpowers and the alliances around them are based on preferences in which patriotism and sovereignty play an important role. These preferences are partly determined by irrational views, as we saw, and partly on misconceptions. It is not clear whether, in these cases, citizens' or governments' preferences need correction, and who or what institution is able to apply the correction. The possibility exists that citizens and governments alike are shortsighted or misled. In that situation the International Court of Justice might be the appropriate institution to correct preferences. In other cases a non-government organisation such as a peace movement, or scientists such as peace researchers may make the correction. The preferences of a part of public opinion expressed by the slogan 'better dead than red' may need such a correction, since it seems to underestimate to a considerable degree the horrors of modern war. Of course a communist who prefers war to living in a capitalist society may also need more information. It is International Physicians for the Prevention of Nuclear War that has to be credited for the information it has provided on modern warfare, and nuclear wars in particular, by pointing out that medical help would fall far short of what would be needed. The Nobel Peace Prize this organisation received in 1985 was quite rightly awarded to them.

At present (1987) it is certain governments' preference rather than the populations' which needs to be corrected.

2.5   MEASUREMENT OF WELFARE AND SECURITY: TWO MODELS

For an integrated welfare and security policy it is important to compare changes in welfare and changes in security that may result from changes in institutions or in policies. Such comparisons can be made with more precision if the concepts of welfare and security have been measured. Within the narrower field of conventional economics the question of the measurability of welfare is a contentious issue. In the last half-century most economists denied the possibility of measuring utility or welfare and followed those who had shown that for a large part of economic science such measurement was not necessary. A number of problems whose solution does require welfare measurement were declared not to be soluble by economic science, but perhaps by other sciences. An important example is the problem of maximising a nation's welfare by income redistribution (through taxation, for instance). The maximum requires the equalisation of marginal welfare, which requires welfare measurement. Alternatively, solutions offered by some authors were declared to be subjective opinions of the author.

In the last decade the number of economists holding the view that welfare is measurable and who are in fact making measurements is increasing. Three groups of authors, an American, a British and a Dutch group, dealt with the problem, and two made measurements. The American group counts among its members Dale W. Jorgenson, Laurits R. Christensen and Lawrence J. Lau. The main publication we are familiar with will be quoted as Jorgenson and Slesnick, 1983. The British group consists of G.W. Mackenzie and I.F. Pearce and their main publication will be quoted as McKenzie, 1983. In contradistinction to the two other groups the British group did not apply its theory to numerical material.

Among the Dutch group, headed by B.M.S. van Praag, we find A. Kapteyn, A. Kouwenhoven, Th. Goedhart, T.J. Wansbeek, F.G. van Herwaarden, J. Buyze and others. The essence of their work consists of direct interviewing of large numbers of European consumers; an example may be found in Van Praag and Kapteyn, 1973. The question refers to welfare attached to the level of income and consists of indicating the income levels at which the interviewees would feel, respectively, excellent, good, sufficient, etc. down to very bad (ten levels). This one-dimensional concept of welfare constitutes one of the simplest approaches, which makes it very appropriate for the purpose of this section. Its one-dimensionality does not imply that the determinants are limited to one determinant only. Fairly satisfactory explanations can be given by five determinants: income after tax, occupation, years of schooling, capability to take independent decisions and age (cf. Tinbergen, 1980).

In view of the 'underdeveloped' character of the concept of security attempts to its measurement may be started with the aid of a similarly simple concept as used by Van Praag in his early attempts to measure welfare. This means that we start with a one-dimensional draft-definition as discussed in section 2.3: the probable extent to which the functioning of its institutions can be chosen by the nation's own inhabitants. The underdeveloped character of the concept of security is reflected in the many questions arising with an analysis of this draft-definition. In fact we present this formulation with the purpose only of generating these questions and will add our own questions with the hope that better questions will be formulated by others. In the tentative approach of this chapter we are going to use the definition of a nation's welfare ω_i chosen in formula (2.2), section 2.2.

We assumed that welfare in the conventional sense ω_i depends on: average income y_i(positively), income inequality z_i(negatively), unemployment u_i(negatively), and an optimal environmental condition e_i(positively). If z_i, u_i and e_i are measured in terms of income conventional welfare, measured in terms of income, will be

$$\omega_i = y_i - z_i - u_i + e_i \tag{2.3}$$

The means considered for the conventional socio-economic order are a choice between three orders, capitalist, mixed and communist, characterised by differing values for y_i, z_i and u_i.

We further assume that the security aspect can be introduced by multiplying ω_i with a factor p_i that we call security or peace probability, itself composed of four multiplicative factors (if the events concerned are independent):

$$p_i = w_i m_i n_i b_i \tag{2.4}$$

where w_i is the probability of peace if decisions about war or peace are made at world level rather than at national levels

m_i is the probability of peace if the ABM-treaty is adhered to

n_i is the probability of peace if the NPT (Non-Proliferation Treaty) is adhered to, and

b_i the probability of peace if a new treaty banning

weapons of mass destruction from outer space is concluded.

Welfare-cum-security ω will then be determined by the formula

$$\omega_i = p\omega_i = w\, m\, n\, b\, (y - z - u + e) \qquad (2.5)$$

In order to measure ω we must have numerical values for all the symbols appearing in this formula. Such values may be obtained from public opinion polls, where the value to be given to y_i must be chosen by the organisers of the poll at 100 for a typically developed country, say the United States, whereas all the other variables must result from the poll.

As an example how this operation may work out we have chosen the values of all variables as follows

y_1 = income under communist regime = 80

y_2 = income under capitalist or mixed regime = 100

z_1 = income inequality under communist or mixed regime = 20

z_2 = income inequality under capitalist regime = 30

u_1 = unemployment under communist regime = 0

u_2 = unemployment under capitalis or mixed regime = 5

e_1 = environment under perfect environmental policy at world level = 10

e_2 = environment under imperfect environmental policy = 0

w_1 = probability of peace if war decisions are made at world level = 1

w_2 = probability of peace if war decisions are made at national level = 0.25

m_1 = probability of peace if ABM treaty is adhered to = 1

m_2 = probability of peace if war decisions are not adhered to = 0.5

n_1 = probability of peace if NPT* is not adhered to = 1

n_2 = probability of peace if NPT is not adhered to = 0.5

b_1 = probability of peace if treaty banning arms in space is concluded = 1

b_2 = probability of peace if treaty banning arms in space is not concluded = 0.1

In Table 2.4 the values of generalised welfare, or welfare-cum-security obtained with formula 2.5 are shown. The security concept involved is the equally tentative 'probability of peace' as expressed in formula (2.4), where quantitative values are shown in Table 2.3.

Obviously our example reflects a number of subjective

NPT stands for Non-Proliferation Treaty

Table 2.4 Values of welfare-cum-security for specified values of its determinants listed above

b	m	n	mnb	e_1 w_1 cap	mix	com	e_1 w_2 cap	mix	com	e_2 w_1 cap	mix	com	e_2 w_2 cap	mix	com
b_2	m_2	n_2	0.025	1.9	2.1	1.8	0.47	0.53	0.44	1.6	1.9	1.5	0.41	0.47	0.38
	m_2	n_1	0.05	3.8	4.3	3.5	0.94	1.06	0.88	3.3	3.8	3.0	0.81	0.94	0.75
	m_1	n_2	0.05	3.8	4.3	3.5	0.94	1.06	0.88	3.3	3.8	3.0	0.81	0.94	0.75
	m_1	n_1	0.1	7.5	8.5	7.0	1.9	2.1	1.8	6.5	7.5	6.0	1.63	1.88	1.50
b_1	m_2	n_2	0.25	18.8	21.3	17.5	4.7	5.3	4.4	16.3	18.8	15.0	4.1	4.7	3.8
	m_2	n_1	0.5	37.5	42.5	35	9.4	10.6	8.8	32.5	37.5	30.0	8.1	9.4	7.5
	m_1	n_2	0.5	37.5	42.5	35	9.4	10.6	8.8	32.5	37.5	30.0	8.1	9.4	7.5
	m_1	n_1	1	75	85	70	19	21	18	65	75	60	16.3	18.8	15.0

Table 2.3 Values of 'probability of peace' or security according to equation (2.2) for the values of its determinants listed before

b	m	n	w_1 (1)	w_2 (0.25)
	m_2	n_2	0.025	0.00625
		n_1	0.05	0.0125
b_2				
	m_1	n_2	0.05	0.0125
		n_1	0.1	0.025
	m_2	n_2	0.25	0.0625
		n_1	0.5	0.125
b_1				
	m_1	n_2	0.5	0.125
		n_1	1	0.25

elements, and the results may vary considerably if the values of the determinants are changed. To begin with the results reflect the authors' preference for a mixed economy, or in political terms, a democratic socialist view. Income inequality is considered a serious drawback, unemployment less serious and a bad environment in between. Here even democratic socialists may have different opinions. Opinions of conservative Americans (at present a majority, but not necessarily in the future) and of communists will deviate from our example.

A diehard preferring death to communism may show values in the 'com' columns twenty times as low as those shown. His opposite number in the SU will reduce to similar figures the 'cap' columns' figures.

, Our choices for y_1 and y_2 should not be rejected on the basis of income estimates for the US and the SU. The two superpowers are not comparable with respect to climate and to level of development. Figures about India and China should also be kept in mind. Perhaps figures about the two German states are the best basis. Moreover variables in the field of human rights should have been introduced.

Our probability of peace figures must be guesswork anyway.

The present section should be seen as an invitation for alternatives and as a starting point for public opinion polls. By ways of example one alternative method of measurement of security may be an attempt to define security as a function of (i) the quantity of the nation's own armament, distinguishing offensive and defensive arms, (ii) the quantity of another nation's weapons, where defensive weapons have a positive and offensive weapons a negative impact, and (iii) non-military variables, for instance the quantity of grain to be supplied by another country.

2.6 A THIRD MODEL

In *Model C* we consider two nations, say the superpowers, with given total national product or income x_i $(i = 1,2)$. They are supposed to spend these incomes on offensive (a_i) and defensive (b_i) arms and on non-military goods and services (y_i), whereas the more prosperous country 1 (the US) is also supposed to transfer to country 2, as a non-military security instrument, an amount v_2. The utility, or welfare-cum-security, function of the two nations is:

$$\omega_1 = 1n(y_1 - v_2 + 1) + \alpha_{11} 1n(a_1 + 1) - \alpha_{12} 1n(a_2 + 1) \quad (2.6)$$
$$+ \beta_{11} 1n(b_1 + 1) + \beta_{12} 1n(b_2 + 1)$$

$$\omega_2 = 1n(y_2 + v_2 + 1) - \alpha_{21} 1n(a_2 + 1) + \alpha_{22} 1n(a_2 + 1) \quad (2.7)$$
$$+ \beta_{21} 1n(b_1 + 1) + \beta_{22} 1n(b_2 + 1)$$

The restrictions imposed on the two countries' spending are:

$$x_1 = y_1 + a_1 + b_1 \quad (2.8)$$
$$x_2 = y_2 + a_2 + b_2 \quad (2.9)$$

and three problems of maximisation will be formulated, I, I' and II.

Problem I assumes that country 1 maximises

$$\omega_1 + \lambda_1 (x_1 - y_1 - a_1 - b_1) \quad (2.10)$$

and country 2 follows country 1 by making $a_2 = a_1$ and $b_2 = b_1$.

Problem I' assumes that country 2 maximises

$$\omega_2 + \lambda_2 (x_2 - y_2 - a_2 - b_2) \quad (2.11)$$

and country 1 follows country 2 by making $a_1 = a_2$ and $b_1 = b_2$
$$(2.12)$$

In these two cases the countries consider themselves completely sovereign.

Problem II assumes that in one way or another, the countries cooperate or shift part of their sovereignty to a supranational organisation in order to maximise their joint welfare-cum-security. Problem II thus consists of maximising

$$\omega_1 + \omega_2 + \lambda_1 (x_1 - y_1 - a_1 - b_1) + \lambda_2 (x_2 - y_2 - a_2 - b_2)$$
$$(2.13)$$

The form of the utility functions has been chosen so as to make the contribution of each of the utility 'factors' equal to zero for a factor amount equal to zero. The coefficients α_{ij} and β_{ij}. where i is the country whose security is affected by arms of country j, may be called the sensitivity of country i with regard to country j's arms, α for offensive and β for defensive weapons. All α and β are positive, implying that offensive arms reduce the other country's security but defensive arms raise it.

REFERENCES

Fischer, D. (1984), 'Weapons technology and the intensity of arms races', *Conflict Management and Peace Science*, Vol. 8, No. 1.

Jorgenson, D.W. and Slesnick, D.T. (1983), '*Inequality in the Distribution of Individual Welfare*', Discussion Paper No. 987, June, Harvard Institute of Economic Research, Harvard University, Cambridge, MA.

Kapteyn, A. (1982), *Nut en economie* (Utility and Economics), Inaugural address, Katholieke Hogeschool (Catholic University), Tilburg, Netherlands.

McKenzie, G.W. (1983), *Measuring Economic Welfare, New Methods*, Cambridge, Cambridge University Press.

Röling, B.V.A. (1985), 'Bewapening, ontwapening, ontwikkeling en veiligheid' (Armament, disarmament, development and security), in B. Goudzwaard (ed.) *Economie, bewapening en ontwikkeling* (Economics, armament and development), Alphen aan den Rijn, Samson Uitgeverij.

Tinbergen, J. (1980), 'Two approaches to quantify the concept of equitable income distribution', *Kyklos* 3, fasc. 1, 3–15.

Van Praag, B.M.S. and A. Kapteyn (1973), 'Further Evidence on the Individual Welfare Function of Income: An Empirical Investigation in the Netherlands', *European Economic Review* 4, 33–62.

3 Optimum Conditions of 'Welfare-Cum-Security'

3.1 OPTIMUM: MAXIMUM WITHIN A FRAMEWORK OF RESTRICTIONS

In this chapter the integrated optimum problem will be dealt with where an optimum 'welfare-cum-security' or 'generalised welfare' is the aim of the policies of two or more countries. As set out in Chapter 1 (section 1.4), the determination of an optimum always requires that we know (i) the aim of the social order and policies in its dependence on its determinants, and (ii) the restrictions which are imposed on society. The solution will be formulated in section 3.8. In the present section the setting of the problem is given.

Two approaches are possible: (a) a simpler approach where security is considered as a good, comparable with a consumer good; and (b) a more complicated approach where security is a state of mind, comparable with welfare, but a collective state of mind for a nation as a whole. In section 2.5 we have interpreted it as the probability of peace (in the minds of the nation's inhabitants). An example of the simpler approach is given by one of us (Fischer, 1984) elsewhere. As observed in section 2.3, more complicated approaches may be desirable where security is a multi-dimensional concept as suggested by polemologists such as Röling. We are operating in a scientific field of rapid development with a potential for readily formulated innovations. In sections 3.2–3.7 the various types of restrictions human society is faced with will be discussed.

3.2 THE NATURAL ENVIRONMENT AS A RESTRICTION

Human activities and hence human society have always been restricted by their natural environment. For most nations, even small ones, the natural environment comprises a complicated set of data, expressed in particular by physical geography. Parts of a nation's territory may be excellent for different agricultural uses. Some areas may be appropriate for the production of a wide range of vegetable crops; others may be more appropriate for animal food production, whether meat or dairy or both. Countries with mountainous regions may be best suited for a variety of products at different altitudes, with corresponding differences in temperature and rainfall, characterising the climates: tropical foodstuffs may be produced as part of the nation's product mix: some tropical goods may be produced in temperate-zone countries in glasshouses. Parts of a mountainous country may be sterile.

Another component of the natural environment consists of the minerals below its surface: ores, or oil and gas deposits. Again the quality of the ores may vary. Many metals from iron to uranium are of great importance to modern industries. The importance of energy for all production underlies the importance of coal, oil and gas deposits. Another energy source is the availability of waterways; here again human intervention may expand capacity by the construction of dams, and similar investments.

It will be obvious that the concept of a natural environment is a highly complicated one whose full significance can only appear in models with a large number of variables.

For a long time the natural environment could be considered as a given, although long-term exhaustion of some natural resources was experienced. Thus, some mineral deposits in Europe have been exhausted and had to be replaced by the exploitations of deposits at greater distances, or substituted by alternative minerals. Iron ore is now being imported from more distant countries; while oil substituted for coal—only to be substituted by coal again after the oil price rises of the 1970s.

In the last decade a new environmental problem of rapidly increasing importance has developed: a changing, and in fact deteriorating quality of some natural resources. This applies to water and air in particular. For a long time pure water and pure air were considered to be freely available and called 'free goods'. There are no restrictions, in other words, to the use of these raw materials or consumer goods. This is no longer true and today restrictions exist on the use of these resources, requiring institutions for the correct management of the limited quantities available. As in many other cases Sweden was the first country to understand the need for international cooperation in this field and offered Stockholm as the meeting place for the 1972 United Nations conference on the subject, resulting in the establishment of the United Nations Environmental Programme (UNEP), with its secretariat in Nairobi, Kenya.

Not only are restrictions on the quantities of pure water and air necessary, but also 'defensive measures' (cf. Leipert, 1984) against pollution of the world's rivers, lakes, seas and atmosphere, causing fish mortality or acid rain threatening our forests.

3.3 HUMAN NATURE AS A RESTRICTION

Not only does the human environment restrict what society can do. We ourselves constitute restrictions on what society can do. To a considerable degree we are creating our own difficulties. In a direct and obvious way this is expressed in what we require for our welfare and our security, and hence in our welfare function and our need for security. In other words, the aim of our social order as a function of its determinants—the coefficients appearing in a welfare function—are among the restrictions.

But, in addition, other human features also restrict our optimal welfare-cum-security: our myopia in time and space being one example. Shortsightedness makes us prefer things we later dislike. This is a valid argument for the correction of some short-term preferences by legislation: well-known examples are compulsory schooling, taxes on unhealthy – and subsidies on healthy ('merit') —goods. It may also be an argument for the correction of national policies by some 'higher' authority, such as a United Nations institution; one example being the International Court of Justice.

Geographic myopia occurs if we concentrate our preferences on national interests instead of continental interests. An example is the pollution of the Rhine by France, until an agreement was reached between all nations affected after which France changed its policy. The same applies to other pollution problems such as the acid rain in Central Europe and Scandinavia. Here Britain, the Netherlands and Belgium may have to follow France's example.

Myopia is not the only attitude damaging our own long-term interest. Rigidity or inertia in thinking is another. Extremists (for instance, communists and conservatives) often tend to rigidity in thinking. It partly coincides with a lack of tolerance.

In order to arrive at an optimal international order we must think creatively and be tolerant. Tolerance is also part of scientific thinking. Marx, who rightly claimed to strive for a scientific socialism, was himself creative; but some of his followers tend to be rigid, non-creative and intolerant. The same applies to the believers in *laissez-faire*, the Manchester liberals (liberals in the European, not the American sense).

Restrictions may also be the effect of a lack of learning capacity, and hence of intelligence. In Chapter 10 the role of learning processes in the broadest sense required for optimal policies, and hence for politicians, will be discussed in more detail.

3.4   TECHNOLOGICAL RESTRICTIONS: CIVILIAN

For the last two centuries human life has been shaped increasingly (and for earlier centuries in a more modest way) by technology. Starting with the simple tools of the Iron Age an ever-expanding exploration of natural resources and creativity in constructing machines, means of transportation and other 'means of production', mankind is now able to produce large quantities of an enormous variety of goods which satisfy its ever-increasing and diversifying needs.

The accumulation of this knowledge and its transmission from one generation to the next is largely in the hands of institutes of technology such as the Massachusetts Institute of Technology (MIT)—probably the most famous among them—and thousands of less well-known institutes. At the same time components of this 'human capital' are to be found in production units (factories, transportation systems, workshops).

Even though the potential for producing all sorts of goods and services is very impressive, there are limits. Any social order must remain within these limits. The economist calls these possibilities *production functions* and these constitute a very important intellectual tool for thinking in concrete terms and for producing 'models' of a social order's qualities. The concept of a production function can be extended to education, especially formal schooling, but also the informal sector: family rearing and training on-the-job. The diversity in schools in today's societies is a reflection of the diversity in our 'production apparatus'.

A distinction must be made between the 'state of the art' of production—that is, the total of technological knowledge of humankind (or the portion available in one country)—and the knowledge and ability of each producing individual. The latter can only command a small part, in which that individual is specialised.

For the purpose of this book we make a distinction between civilian production and security production. They share a large common territory, but also have a considerable specialised area. One relationship between the latter two is of particular relevance to this book: the concept of *conversion*. By this term we indicate the transformation of a production unit (a factory, for instance) producing military goods into one producing civilian goods. A simple example is the transformation of a tank into a tractor factory.

3.5 TECHNOLOGICAL RESTRICTIONS: SECURITY

Further restrictions originate in the security sector. Here too many production processes are used, characterised by their production functions. A number of military goods may be distinguished, depending on the degree of detail chosen in the model used. Two aspects are of particular interest: (i) What differences in technological knowledge exist between the parties in conflict? And (ii) What uncertainties exist in the technologies used by the other party now or in the future?

It is a commonplace that the two superpowers each has its stronger and its weaker capabilities. Thus, the US is more advanced in electronic devices, sea-based systems and in satellites (even though the SU was first in this field in 1957 with Sputnik). The SU, in contrast, is more advanced in laser beams, and in mass production of simpler arms: the Warsaw Pact countries produce about twice the number of tanks, five times the number of ballistic missiles and twelve times as many guns as NATO members (1983 figures) (cf. Berkhof, 1985; Holloway, 1985; Stares, 1985).

Uncertainties about the other party's arms exist in particular with regard to arms concealed below sea-level or otherwise, or mobile arms. Uncertainties may also be due to new experiences or insights: the opinion on the efficiency of MIRVs (multiple independently targetable re-entry vehicles) has changed completely; a number of defensive systems were later dismantled.

The greatest uncertainties exist, as a matter of course, about possible future technological development. This is particularly acute with regard to the Strategic Defence Initiative (SDI) proposed by President Reagan in 1983 and made a major point of negotiation in the preparation of the November 1985 meeting in Geneva of General Secretary Gorbachev and President Reagan. SDI is based on the belief that a technological defence against missile attacks will become possible within five to ten years of intensive research. Most independent American and most Soviet experts are highly sceptical about this. Even so military planners must always reckon with the worst conceivable alternative; and if the other party invents an effective defence technology this would give it first-strike capability: this is the reason why Soviet opposition to SDI has been so strong. The only answer then consists of as great an increase as possible in offensive, known technology.

3.6   BALANCE EQUATIONS AND DEFINITIONS

The societal process we are describing is characterised by the feature that each element of any society (human beings of various sorts, goods and services of all kinds) has an origin and a destination. The quantities 'created' must be equal to the quantities 'used', plus those left in stock. For products this is clear. For human beings it may mean (in a macro-model) that in each time unit births are equal to deaths plus the 'increase in population plus the emigration balance'. In a micro-model, similar relations apply to all specified sub-groups, according to age, sex, occupation, territory and so on. The relations discussed are known as *balance equations*.

Another type of 'self-evident' relations among the restrictions are so-called *definition equations*. A very simple example is that the value of a quantity of some good equals quantity × price. Such relations need not occur as restrictions if the value is replaced by the product of quantity and price. The model-builder is free to omit one of the variables and the definition of the variable in terms of other variables used. Such elimination is often possible, but sometimes difficult or even impossible and so is part of the scientific strategy chosen.

3.7 ADHERENCE OR NON-ADHERENCE TO TREATIES

In one of the methods chosen in section 2.5 to deal with the concept of security a qualitative restriction was introduced, namely the adherence or non-adherence to one (or more) treaties. Since this is an important form of peace policy it is worthwhile introducing it *expressis verbis* in a separate section. Methodologically it is important also, since it constitutes a method to deal with problems that at present can only be treated qualitatively.

Treaties are obtained by *negotiations*. This important diplomatic activity may be considered as a production process. A particularly interesting example is the nine-year negotiation that within the framework of the United Nations led to the new Law of the Sea. Systematic research on negotiation as a technique is being done in the framework of the International Institute for Applied Systems Analysis (IIASA) in Laxenburg, Austria.

3.8 OPTIMUM CONDITIONS AND THEIR INTERPRETATION

After having discussed the restrictions under which welfare-cum-security has to be maximised we now consider what conditions the means used by the national societies have to satisfy, in order that these societies constitute optimal structure and pursue optimal policies.

In the most general treatment of our problem the institutions which as a set constitute the optimal order we are searching for are the problem's unknowns. The optimum conditions (conditions for a maximum welfare-cum-security), obtained for a full-fledged quantitative model with the aid of some mathematical methods have to be interpreted as the operation of a number of institutions, which then are the set we are searching for. This interpretation also constitutes the essence of what is known as welfare economics.

Sometimes quantification is not necessary and the qualitative treatment suffices. In other cases it is not yet possible. Mathematical methods have to be used if quantitative approaches are desirable and feasible. There is a choice between various methods, known as mathematical programming and Lagrange multipliers. These may be interpreted as the prices on competitive markets, implying a prohibition of non-competitive (oligopolistic or monopolistic) markets or the levying of import duties, excise duties, etc. and quantitative restrictions (quotas). In order to understand the structure, figures are not always needed: prices of individual goods will change and within limits are irrelevant; Tax rates, however, may be important.

The most general treatment described requires creativity to find the institutions fitting a given set of optimum conditions. The same conditions may be fulfilled by free competition markets and by planning: planned prices and quantities *can* be chosen equal to free competition prices.

Almost the same creativity can be used by proposing some preconceived institutions, though. In Table 2.1 the preconceived institutions are adherence to certain treaties. So here the restrictions are already expressed in terms of institutions and applying the restrictions simply means blocking part of Table 2.2. Another example of such a simple non-mathematical procedure will be discussed in section 4.9 and is part of a very important aspect we shall call the *optimum level of decision-making*.

3.9   OPTIMUM CONDITIONS IN MODELS A AND C

For Model A, Problem I, the restrictions are merely that each country's total inputs at the beginning of a production period must not exceed the total outputs available at the end of the previous period, for each sector of the economy. The goal is to maximise the sustainable growth rate of the economy, which is the lowest growth rate of any sector.

Since the growth rate is unchanged if all inputs and outputs are multiplied by a constant factor, we can, without loss of generality, assume that the quantity of civilian goods available at the beginning of the current period is one unit. The amount allocated to the military industry is denoted by μ_1 and the remainder, $1 - \mu_1$, is allocated to the civilian industry. It would not be efficient to use less than the total available amount of civilian goods for all inputs. Country 2, which starts out with an equal amount of resources, allocates μ_2 to its military industry and $1 - \mu_2$ to its civilian industry. The resulting growth factors (= output/input) for each sector are as follows:

Table 3.1

Sector	Civilian	Security
Input	$(1 - \mu_1) + \mu_1 =$	$d\mu_2$
Output	1	$c\mu_1$
Growth factor	$b(1 - \mu_1)$	$c\mu_1/d\mu_2$
	$b(1 - \mu_1)$	

In the optimum, the lower of these two growth rates is a maximum.

For Problem II, the amount μ of civilian goods at the global level is allocated to the military industry, and $1 - \mu$ to the civilian industry. The growth rates are

Table 3.2

Sector	Civilian	Security
Input	$(1 - \mu) + \mu = 1$	$d\mu$
Output	$b(1 - \mu)$	$c\mu$
Growth Factor	$b(1 - \mu)$	c/d

The optimum conditions which have to be satisfied in Model C have to be obtained by putting the first derivatives of the expression (2.10) with regard to each of the unknowns equal to zero for the solutions of Problem I, those of the expression (2.11) for Problem I' and those of both (2.10) and (2.11) for Problem II.

For Problem I this means that:

$$\partial\omega_1/\partial y_1 - \lambda_1 = 0 \qquad (3.1)$$
$$\partial\omega_1/\partial a_1 - \lambda_1 = 0 \qquad (3.2)$$
$$\partial\omega_1/\partial b_1 - \lambda_1 = 0 \qquad (3.3)$$
$$\partial\omega_1/\partial v_2 \quad\quad = 0 \qquad (3.4)$$

Similarly, for Problem I we must have:

$$\partial\omega_2\partial y_2 - \lambda_2 = 0 \qquad (3.5)$$
$$\partial\omega_2/\partial a_2 - \lambda_2 = 0 \qquad (3.6)$$
$$\partial\omega_2/\partial b_2 - \lambda_2 = 0 \qquad (3.7)$$
$$\partial\omega_2/\partial v_2 \quad\quad = 0 \qquad (3.8)$$

For Problem II the optimum conditions are:

$$\partial(\omega_1 + \omega_2)/\partial y_1 - \lambda_1 = 0 \qquad (3.9)$$
$$\partial(\omega_1 + \omega_2)/\partial a_1 - \lambda_1 = 0 \qquad (3.10)$$
$$\partial(\omega_1 + \omega_2)/\partial b_1 - \lambda_1 = 0 \qquad (3.11)$$

$$\partial(\omega_1 + \omega_2)/\partial y_2 - \lambda_2 = 0 \qquad (3.12)$$
$$\partial(\omega_1 + \omega_2)/\partial a_2 - \lambda_2 = 0 \qquad (3.13)$$
$$\partial(\omega_1 + \omega_2)/\partial b_2 - \lambda_2 = 0 \qquad (3.14)$$
$$\partial(\omega_1 + \omega_2)/\partial v_2 \qquad = 0 \qquad (3.15)$$

In addition the restrictions (2.65) or (2.66) or both must be satisfied.

REFERENCES

Berkhof, G.C. (1985), 'President Reagan's SDI', *Atl. Perspect.*, 2, 9–16.

Fischer, D. (1984), 'Weapons Technology and the Intensity of Arms Races', *Conflict Management and Peace Science* 8, 49–69.

Holloway, D. (1985), 'The Strategic Defense Initiative and the Soviet Union', *Daedalus*, Summer, 114, No. 3, 257–78.

Leipert, C. (1984), 'Bruttosozialprodukt, defensive Ausgaben und Nettowohlfahrtsmessung' [GNP, defensive expenditures and net welfare measurement], *Zeitschrift für Umweltpolitik* 7, H 3, 229–55.

Stares, P. (1985), 'US and Soviet Military Space Programmes: A Comparative Assessment', *Daedalus*, Spring, 114, No. 2, 127–45.

4 The Optimal Social Order: Its Means and Institutions

4.1 OPTIMAL SOCIAL ORDER

In this chapter a description of the optimal order is offered as seen by different scholars belonging to different schools of thought and reflected by differences in political convictions. We offer our own interpretation of these views which are not necessarily as they are seen by the scholars in question. In other words, we try to make understandable why differences in political convictions are possible as long as scientific research is not perfect and has not proved beyond doubt the mistaken assumptions made by some schools of thought. Of course we are aware of the possibility and even probability that assumptions falsified by scientific research and no longer adhered to by any scholar may still be held by the public and politicians. Scientific results need a long time to penetrate public opinion and are often opposed by the people and politicians if they threaten the latters' interests.

On the other hand, a number of propositions may be so self-evident that they are held by virtually everybody, whatever their political allegiance. We believe that such propositions exist in the fields covered by our subject and that their number can be increased. World opinion seems to be approaching the conviction that a nuclear war cannot be won and that therefore nuclear weapons cannot and must not be used. The full consequences of this belief are not yet clear.

In the present chapter the most important features of an optimum order will be discussed, but not the way to attain it: that subject will be dealt with in Chapters 9 and 10 of Part II.

For a clear understanding of the main features of an optimal order a minimum number of nations must be considered. The social order in the conventional sense can be studied for single countries. In the sense that it is understood in this book, where the security element is included, at least two countries or two alliances must be studied; if we want to combine this with the problem of development cooperation we must consider at least three 'worlds', as illustrated by the use of the phrase 'Third World'.

A basic feature on which differences exist between various schools of socio-economic research is the degree of centralisation in decision-making needed in an optimal economic order. Those who believe strongly in the self-regulatory capability of the economy are in favour of a relatively small number of means or instruments. The typical example is the school of *laissez-faire*, represented today by the conservatives in the US and in Europe, as well as in a number of developing countries: this applies to the political party or parties in power, and not of course to the opposition. At the other extreme we have the communist-ruled countries, where the leading scholars emphasise the need for a large number of instruments, operating in a system of central planning, and hence a high degree of centralisation of decision-making.

An intermediate position is held by scholars and politicians known as democratic socialists. Their optimal order is often called a *mixed economy*, since it combines a considerable, but not excessive, degree of public intervention with self-regulation of a considerable number of sectors or markets. Comparable, but somewhat more conservative, opinions are held by Christian Democrats and European Liberals.

There is no generally agreed opinion about the relative success of these three main schools. It depends on the criteria used which system is best. Serious observers of the various systems admit that some features in each of the three main orders are better than others. Thus, the overwhelming problem of unemployment constitutes a disqualification of both the capitalist and the mixed systems. Income inequality also constitutes a less favourable characteristic of the capitalist system (cf. Wiles, 1978). In contrast, the average level of prosperity is clearly higher in capitalist societies, associated with greater opportunities for enterprising individuals. The disadvantage of unemployment in the mixed system is partly compensated by the unemployment benefits paid to the jobless. A serious drawback of the communist systems is their authoritarian character, in particular the way in which citizens with dissenting opinions are treated.

4.2 CIVILIAN INSTITUTIONS AND THEIR INSTRUMENTS

In the following sections the institutions and their instruments will be described whose operation is directed at a maximum of traditional welfare, disregarding security. A distinction is made between planning institutions and executive institutions, whose relative importance differs considerably between centrally planned and market economies. In the present section we discuss this choice of the *degree of centralisation* or intensity of central planning. The choice should depend on an evaluation of the advantages and the disadvantages of central planning.

The *advantages* are: (a) that central planning may help to avoid large-scale inconsistencies between important decisions about how to develop an economy. Market economies (or capitalist societies) suffer, periodically, from the consequences of inconsistencies in investment decisions, which may lead to over-capacity in some industrial activities, in particular new activities. During the nineteenth and the twentieth centuries market economies have shown various types of cyclical movements, the avoidance of which will be discussed in more detail in Chapter 6. These cycles brought unemployment of sometimes considerable numbers of workers, losses to enterprises, and other socially undesirable phenomena which rarely occur in centrally planned or communist societies.

Another advantage of central planning is that it enables a country to choose from a larger number of policies: central planning may be directed at the prices and quantities of goods and services that would obtain under free competition, but it may also be directed at numerous other developments: it is not forced to move along the capitalist path, but has considerable flexibility.

Central planning also has its disadvantages. First, it requires a number of workers at various levels of skill, including large numbers of economists, engineers and other academically trained workers, who are not available for other, perhaps more useful, purposes. In the large bureaucracy in which they work conflicts may arise about competence and methods of work, resulting in rigidity in decision-making. In the history of central planning we find examples of rather primitive methods being used. The so-called input–output method used in the early periods of planning in the SU was primitive: production figures were chosen arbitrarily, and consumption treated as a residual; contrasting with the more sophisticated methods developed by the American economist (of Russian origin) W. Leontief. Finally, central planning may be performed in ways whose effects initially look very promising, but eventually work out undesirably, because of over-ambitious targets. One example is what J. Kornai calls 'rush growth' (Kornai, 1971).

The choice of the optimal quantity and quality of central planning made by various economists, politicians or citizens obviously depends on the relative evaluation of these and other advantages and disadvantages of central planning and varies between such widely different systems as used in the two superpowers, which are close to the extremes to be found in economics literature. Of course, the choices change with success-ive governments. The US under Franklin D. Roosevelt was radically different from Ronald Reagan's US. China in 1986 is very different from under Mao.

Most European countries are in favour of a degree of central planning which falls between that of the superpowers; but variations exist and the differences between Scandinavian coun-tries and Mrs Thatcher's UK are considerable. Yet, the European average is closer to what may be called a mixed economy (as mentioned in Chapter 2, especially section 2.5).

One way of characterising the various shades of central planning is to emphasise the way of storing the information necessary for managing the economy: central planning adherents prefer centralised storage while market economy adherents prefer storage spread over all enterprises with only minor portions in Central Statistical Bureaux and the Ministries.

4.3   PLANNING INSTITUTIONS

As observed, nations in favour of a high degree of centralisation and a large number of means of socio-economic policy are characterised by an extensive planning apparatus. This apparatus is structured hierarchically: at the lowest level planning units exist in single production units and at the highest level a central planning unit is in charge of coordinating the production processes of all production units. In other words, the planning machinery reflects the structure of production with its raw materials, intermediate products and products in the retail distribution system facing the prospective consumers. It shares with the production system its ramifications and linkages, and in particular its division into consumer goods and services and investment goods and services. It also shares with the production system its geographical distribution. The most important inputs into a planning process are human effort, information inputs and research orders. Its main capital goods are buildings and computers. (For planning as a production process, see Tinbergen, 1964.)

This picture does not apply to planning in mixed societies. The links between the elements of such a planning system are hardly comparable to a hierarchy, being voluntary rather than imposed. The central planning office publishes research results in the form of reports, and is available for information; it may also accept research commissions from the government and research inquiries from all sorts of institutions: political parties, research institutes, trade unions, employers' associations and so on. The plans drawn up are not imposed on production units but may serve as a guideline; they are known as *indicative plans*.

For planning at the *world level* econometric models are needed which, in principle, reflect the main features of the world economy. In the United Nations Secretariat in New York a first attempt to construct such a model was developed by Jacob L. Mosak, but never published. It was used frequently for many of the Secretariat's tasks, and was particularly useful for the work of the United Nations Development Planning Committee, established in 1966.

In 1968 an international research programme was established, known as *Project Link*, in which models for a large number of market economies were combined with a model for most of the non-communist world. Models for the developing world were taken care of by UNCTAD (cf. Ball, 1973; Waelbroeck, 1976). Shortly after 1970 a large demand for its use developed following the end of the Bretton Woods System and, a little later, the oil price rises imposed by OPEC.

Both Mosak's model and *Project Link* are economic models in the traditional sense: security aspects are not covered. This is undertaken by the Berlin Science Centre in its *Model Globus* (cf. Deutsch, 1984).

4.4 EXECUTIVE INSTITUTIONS FOR PRODUCTION, DISTRIBUTION AND CONSUMPTION

Now we come to the heart of our subject: what institutions are required in order to realise the optimal conditions which must be satisfied to make welfare as great as possible within the framework of the restrictions mankind is subject to. In the preceding section we saw that the number of institutions is much larger in communist-ruled than in market economies as a consequence of differences on the degree that automatic regulation is able to approach a maximum of welfare. We shall discuss the two main types of social order, but arrive at the conclusion that there is a range of orders rather than only two opposed ones. The education system will be discussed separately in section 4.5.

A centrally planned society consists of a close-knit system of institutions arranged hierarchically with such strong interconnections that rigidity is almost unavoidable. We pointed out that a parallel exists between the planning institutions and the executive institutions. The executive institutions together are a machinery that starts operations after the plan has been approved and the planning period started. These operations are dovetailed as much as possible and so fewer inconsistencies occur than in market economies, but also fewer spontaneous responses to unexpected events are possible; such responses take longer than in a market economy, because the decisions must be made at the top. In particular when the unexpected event takes place at a low level the information has to follow a long chain up and down. Still, this only applies to the more important activities and the decisions they need. And even in existing centrally planned economies large numbers of minor decisions are made in the workplace or at some intermediate level.

Moreover, in these economies a number of important activities are unregulated, such as some personal services, agriculture on small private plots whose products are sold in the free market. Also the system of central planning has been changed several times and the number of criteria a production unit has to satisfy has been reduced. The spatial structure constitutes another element where a choice must be made between different possibilities (cf. Chapter 5).

Market economies, which we shall treat as a type of order opposed to centrally planned economies, prefer a minimum of 'concrete' and a maximum of 'abstract' institutions such as markets and 'absence of intervention' (or 'freedom'). That minimum of concrete institutions consists of the most restricted form of government performing a number of policing tasks, such as the prevention of illegal activities (theft, violence against persons and their property, restriction of competition, etc.) or 'internal security'. Another task of such a government may be described as the management of collective (or public) goods, whose consumption by one person cannot prevent consumption by other individuals. Private management—although conceivable—seems inappropriate. In order to decide about the use or production of collective goods, the utility to all citizens must be estimated and this constitutes a community task. A typical collective good is the 'mobile environment'—the atmosphere, the seas and rivers—protection against floods has been considered a government task for centuries. In modern societies not only dykes to prevent flooding, but also the transportation infrastructure, and many types of information (from libraries, statistical offices, radio and television broadcasting) are examples of collective goods.

This most restricted form of government may, however, be non-optimal if the operation of the abstract institutions of markets do not satisfy the optimality conditions. In particular, the optimum condition of *equal marginal welfare* of all citizens requires an income distribution that does not obtain. This requires a taxation system producing equal marginal welfare. Such a system must differentiate between citizens of different family size, with different health and employment prospects. In brief, important elements of what we call a *social security system* must be present.

So the most restricted system of government appears, on closer inspection, to be more elaborate than proponents of *laissez-faire* imagine. This applies also to what we called prevention of the restriction of competition. Known as anti-trust or anti-cartel policy, this government task also is less simple than may be thought. This may be illustrated by Dutch legislation. This is based on a closer analysis of the phenomenon of cartelisation. This analysis shows that in some industries or in some periods unlimited competition may lead to prices resulting in permanent losses for all enterprises of a branch of industry ('cut-throat competition'). Dutch legislation prescribes that in such cases cartelisation has to be imposed in order to assure continuity of production, whereas in other cases cartel-building has to be prohibited.

Another example of markets which do not satisfy the optimum conditions are *unstable markets*, that is markets whose random disturbances are not followed by a quick re-establishment of equilibrium. This may be due to long lags in the reactions of demand or supply, to inelasticity of both supply and demand, or by speculators' activities. In today's world a number of *commodity agreements* have been concluded in order to regulate some of these markets (tin, wheat, rubber, coffee, cocoa, sugar, olive oil, jute and tropical timber). For a useful summary of how these agreements had worked until 1985, cf. UNCTAD (1985).

These examples show that the optimal social system is not one of two alternatives only: a 'socialist' and a 'capitalist'. There is an almost continuous range of systems between the two. Only the extremes do not exist. This point of view has been expressed clearly by Adler Karlsson (1967). The relative importance of government intervention varies from little (in the US) to considerable (in the SU) with many intermediate positions, in general from Southern to Northern Europe: the Scandinavian countries having quite a lot, as, in another way, does Yugoslavia. Recently in China a rather important shift has taken place. Within Eastern Europe (the Council of Mutual Economic Aid, CMEA countries) there are differences also, with Hungary having somewhat less intervention than Bulgaria, for instance.

The existence of this range shows that preferences vary among nations, because of historical, geographical and cultural differences and makes it easier for all nations to understand each other. If explained to the public this may be used to reduce distrust and be used to raise security.

4.5   THE FORMAL EDUCATION SYSTEM

We have excluded one set of institutions from description so far, the *formal education system*: the system of all schools, whose task is to transfer to the younger generation the knowledge and capabilities thought to be desirable. Subdividing a nation's population into annual cohorts indicates that each year an old generation leaves productive life and a younger one enters it. More generally, deaths and births, and emigration and immigration also contribute to a gradual takeover by the younger from the older and in part by foreigners from nationals, or vice versa. Here we restrict ourselves to the formal education system; i.e. informal education within the family, by friends and at work is largely left out of consideration. For the inclusion of the education system into an optimal order cf. Tinbergen (1985).

In many countries a distinction is made between *primary*, *secondary* and *tertiary* education for children of different ages and different capabilities and interests. Another distinction is that between *general* and *vocational* training. Part of schooling, at present mostly primary and secondary, is obligatory. Youngsters with high levels of intelligence or other capabilities will be encouraged, and mostly also prefer, to go on to tertiary education. This is specialised and implies a preparation for the future job(s). Formal education usually ends by taking exams. This constitutes some sort of screening, facilitating a future employer's selection. However learning process does not finish, but goes on informally and each individual's capabilities are enriched by practical experience. The process of selection goes on too and in this process leading personalities in all walks of life come to the fore. Like every human activity the processes of education, selection and finding a permanent position do not happen without mistakes. Pupils or students may be not correctly assessed; or they may themselves not know what they are able to do or what will satisfy them. The art of teaching has been an ongoing subject of research and in the course of the last centuries important improvements have been made. The effect of teaching depends on the student's attitudes also, however, and not only on the individual student's but also on classroom behaviour. The latter seems to change over time, cyclically as well as trendwise. Much remains unexplained.

The general educational level of the population may be considered a collective good and hence subject to government supervision. Even if private and church schools are part of a country's system, they will be supervised. This supervision often extends beyond school education and covers the practical training organised by production units (training on the job), which usually has to satisfy a number of conditions.

Part of education is devoted, of course, to the development of non-intellectual development: to moral or ethical development. As a rule this also contains a preparation for life in the country's social order. There are differences between countries in the intensity of the indoctrination implied in this aspect of schooling. Western countries show a higher degree of tolerance *vis-à-vis* other orders or at least *vis-à-vis* teachers adhering to another social order. In communist countries less tolerance is allowed which may be seen by future generations as a less desirable feature in the long run.

4.6   SECURITY INSTITUTIONS: POLITICAL

As observed, security may be raised by military or by non-military institutions. The latter may be called *political* institutions and consist primarily of the institutions of the Ministry of Foreign Affairs (in the US the State Department) which coordinates all diplomatic contacts, deals with the nation's membership of international organisations and the nation's adherence to a number of treaties. In addition there are other ministries handling international contacts. Foreign trade constitutes a very important instrument, and so do financial and monetary transactions. Ministries with different names in various countries deal with the former issue and the Ministry of Finance (or the Treasury) with the latter. Trade policies are a very important instrument that can be used to the advantage but also strongly to the disadvantage of other countries. Thus, prohibiting the exports of new technology, such as electronics devices, may negatively affect the relation between the exporting and the would-be importing country. Continuing the exports of wheat to the SU was, in contrast, a positive gesture by the US.

The role that may be played by non-military institutions in an attempt to influence a country's security favourably was illustrated particularly clearly by our Model C (sections 2.6 and 3.9); we shall discuss this in sections 4.8 and 4.9.

A particularly important set of political institutions contributing to security is the machinery used by the member states of the European Community with the general purpose of integrating them into one union, comparable to the superpowers, except for the overdevelopment of their armed forces. This integration process serves both the socio-economic and the security interests of the member nations. To generalise it may be stated that enlargement of the market will raise prosperity as a consequence of economies of scale and of specialisation, but also by the elimination of a considerable number of unnecessary activities, such as frontier checks of all sorts of documents, and transformations of all kinds because of different traditions, legislation and systems of standardisation.

But of especial importance is the enhancement of security, in particular the reduction of the possibility of an armed conflict between France and Germany, which occurred in 1870–71, 1914–18 and 1939–45.

It should be emphasised that in other parts of the world, and eventually in the whole world, this is a possible approach to enhancing security. This is the reason why it is mentioned: Europe offers examples which may be instructive to other continents and to the world at large. Unfortunately examples of how *not* to do things also can be found.

Finally, the International Court of Justice, located in The Hague, should be mentioned as an institution capable of raising security, on the condition, of course, that its competence is recognised. The recent attitude shown by the present American administration does not constitute an intelligent policy.

4.7 SECURITY INSTITUTIONS: MILITARY

In the pre-nuclear era military institutions were used, by the stronger and more aggressive nations, in order to raise their welfare or security, or what they thought was welfare-cum-security, if political means did not work as they wanted. Armed conflicts were considered to be 'the continuation of diplomacy by other means'. However one evaluates such decisions (much can be argued against the use of arms in the pre-nuclear era), they have to be revised as a consequence of the existence of nuclear arms, since these arms cannot be used; their function is said to be to *deter*, but the true meaning of that phrase is not clear and accordingly military thinking has become inconsistent. This constitutes an autonomous argument against military thinking and activity.

As long as we restrict ourselves to non-nuclear weapons, this additional argument does not apply and military thinking can be consistent. Then, the distinction between *offensive* and *defensive* weapons makes sense for part of today's arms. Following many others we state that offensive weapons may increase the owner's security but reduce the other party's, whereas in some situations defensive weapons enhance *both parties'* security.

Unfortunately we have taken over from Hitler the development of rockets, which are offensive in by far the larger number of applications. Where we have developed defensive arms as a counterpart to offensive arms (anti-tank guns, anti-aircraft guns, etc.), (on both sides) we have only very imperfect defensive weapons to counter a missile (rocket) attack, notwithstanding the research programmes made so far, on both sides. The optimum level of security will be characterised by defensive weapons available to authorities which do not want to attack. The weak point in such an optimum remains the uncertainty about the other side's intentions. Both the US and the SU by their past behaviour give rise to doubts about their intentions.

Perhaps some comfort can be derived from Baer-Kaupert's (1985) statement that 'the intention to attack can be read into military planning only if supporting evidence can be found in the *security policy as a whole*. At the present time, in both East and West, there is no such evidence'. But, as Fischer points out, the only way one can fully trust a declaration of no offensive intentions is if the party making that statement is *unable*, with the arms it has, to attack.

We are far from this situation, however, and both sides will take into account the possibility of the other side's first-strike capability as soon as a near-perfect defensive counterpart to missiles has been found. For this reason most independent experts advise that a race in searching for such counterparts be blocked by a new treaty preventing the use of weapons in outer space. An alternative is to develop, in full cooperation with the other party, all new knowledge so as to attain common security (Palme, 1982). This sounds unrealistic but it is correct that an actual technology for a near-perfect defence against missiles would constitute a higher level of security.

Some American civil servants seem to share this opinion (cf. Spoor, 1985). This aim seems attainable only after both parties have convincingly shown they are not *able* to attack, hence a large-scale *verifiable destruction* of present offensive armament is needed. While this remains the 'optimum optimorum', for the time being the optimum seems to be to ban all weapons from outer space.

4.8 THE INTEGRATED OPTIMAL SOCIAL ORDER

The solution of the main problem Part I of this book deals with (to identify the social order which in the long run tends to maximise world welfare-cum-security) can be obtained in the way set out in the preceding sections of this chapter. In this and the following section we shall illustrate this by using the Models A, B and C of Chapter 2 (sections 2.2, 2.5 and 2.6). We start with Model A.

For Problem I: Country 1 faces the following dilemma: the larger the fraction μ_1 of its civilian goods it allocates to the civilian economy, the faster its civilian economy grows, but the less secure it will be if it is threatened by an adversary. The more it allocates to the military industry, the more secure it will generally be, but the lower is the growth of its economy, and in the end it will not even be able to sustain the production of arms, if its civilian economy lags behind. It is assumed that it will seek a solution of balanced growth, where the slowest growing sector grows as fast as possible. In general, this will imply that all sectors grow at the same rate.

It can be seen that if μ_1 is chosen so as to maximise the lesser of the two growth factors in Table 3.1, the two growth factors are equal:

$$b(1 - \mu_1) = c\mu_1/d\mu_2,$$

or

$$\mu_1 = \mu_2/(\mu_2 + c/bd)$$

Since country 2 faces the same problem, we also have:

$$\mu_2 = \mu_1/(\mu_1 + c/bd)$$

Using the abbreviation $e = c/bd$ and inserting μ_2 in the expression for μ_1 yields a quadratic equation $\mu_1^2 - (1 - e)\mu_1 = 0$ with the two solutions:

$$\mu_1 = \mu_2 = 1 - e$$

or

$$\mu_1 = \mu_2 = 0$$

Each of those two solutions represents a Cournot–Nash equilibrium. To see whether these equilibria are stable, we calculate the first derivative

$$d\mu_1/d\mu_2 = e/(\mu_1 + e)^2$$

If this derivative is greater than 1, a small deviation in the arms expenditures of country 2 from the equilibrium level will induce country 1 to undertake an even larger change, and vice versa by symmetry. This means that the equilibrium is unstable. The slightest deviation leads to a progressive race away from it. If the derivative is less than 1, the equilibrium is stable.

Since $d\mu_1/d\mu_2 = 1/e$ if $\mu_2 = 0$
and $d\mu_1/d\mu_2 = e$ if $\mu_2 = 1 - e$,

we can observe that

if $e < 1$, $\mu_1 = \mu_2 = 1 - e$ is a stable equilibrium and

$$\mu_1 = \mu_2 = 0 \qquad \text{is an unstable equilibrium.}$$
If $e > 1$, $\mu_1 = \mu_2 = 0$ \qquad is a stable equilibrium and
$$\mu_1 = \mu_2 = 1 - e \text{ is an unstable equilibrium.}$$

For Problem II, we see from Table 3.2 that the growth factors are b $(1 - \mu)$ for civilian goods , and c/d for security (if the military industry is operated with positive intensity) or indeterminate (if $\mu = 0$, i.e. if no arms are produced). The optimal solution in this case is not to produce any weapons at all, and to allow the civilian economy to grow from each period to the next with the maximum feasible growth factor b for $\mu = 0$.

The Von Neumann growth model permits solutions in which not all industrial sectors are operated with a positive intensity, and not all goods produced and used. For a detailed description of the Von Neumann growth model, see Morgenstern and Thompson (1976). For the treatment of externalities in such a model, see Fischer (1977).

Now Model B will be used for illustration. Model B is not a fully quantitative model, since its variables can only assume discrete values. The impact on welfare-cum-security of its variables is shown in Table 2.2. The restrictions take the form of excluding groups of cells of this table. If environmental policy is decided on at world level, only the left-hand half of Table 2.2 is valid; if an imperfect environmental policy is followed, only the right-hand half is valid. If the ABM Treaty is adhered to, only the rows where $m = m_1$ are valid within the left-hand or right-hand half. The optimum solution can then be read from the lowest line of the table, meaning that we must have $w = w_1$ (decision on armed conflict at world level), $n = n_1$ (Non-Proliferation Treaty adhered to) and $b = b_1$ (a treaty banning arms in space is concluded).

Taking up Model C (cf. section 2.6) now, which is fully quantitative, the restrictions are introduced with the aid of Lagrange multipliers and the model expressed in a set of equations (section 3.9).

Problems I, I' as introduced there constitutes the order where the two superpowers follow a sovereign policy; and Problem II the order where they behave as members of an ideal 'United Nations' aiming at common welfare and common security.

We shall illustrate our example in three stages. First, we give the general solutions, then we add a numerical elaboration. Finally we offer a verbal interpretation (in section 4.9).

The general solution to Problem I must consist of four

equations for the four unknowns (and one equation to eliminate the Lagrange multiplier). Upon closer inspection it appears that (3.4) cannot be satisfied: it would require that $y_1 - v_1 = \infty$. This means that the maximum with regard to v_2 cannot be a flat maximum, but has to be a boundary maximum. In the present case we choose $v_2 = 0$. Introducing this value as given and carrying out the differentiations we obtain, after elimination of λ_1:

$$a_1 + 1 = \alpha_{11}(y_1 + 1) \tag{4.1}$$
$$b_1 + 1 = \beta_{11}(y_1 + 1) \tag{4.2}$$
$$y_1 + 1 = (x_1 + 3)/(1 + \alpha_{11} + \beta_{11}) \tag{4.3}$$

In Problem I' too we must reject equation (3.8) since it requires that $y_2 + v_2 = \infty$. Moreover, it is not in the power of Country 2 to choose v_2; it seems more realistic also here to take $v_2 = 0$. We are then left with:

$$a_2 + 1 = \alpha_{22}(y_2 + 1) \tag{4.4}$$
$$b_2 + 1 = \beta_{22}(y_2 + 1) \tag{4.5}$$
$$y_2 + 1 = (x_2 + 3)/(1 + \alpha_{22} + \beta_{22}) \tag{4.6}$$

Problem II has seven unknowns and after elimination of the λ_1 and λ_2 we obtain the following seven equations:

$$a_1 + 1 = (\alpha_{11} - \alpha_{21})(y + 1) \tag{4.7}$$
$$b_1 + 1 = (\beta_{11} + \beta_{21})(y + 1) \tag{4.8}$$
$$a_2 + 1 = (\alpha_{22} - \alpha_{12})(y + 1) \tag{4.9}$$
$$b_2 + 1 = (\beta_{12} + \beta_{22})(y + 1) \tag{4.10}$$
$$y_1 - v_2 = y_2 + v_2 = y \tag{4.11}$$

$$v_2 = \frac{1}{2}(x_1 - x_2)$$

$$- \frac{1}{2}(\alpha_{11} - \alpha_{21} - \alpha_{22} + \alpha_{12} + \beta_{11} + \beta_{21} - \beta_{12} - \beta_{22}) \tag{4.12}$$

where the variable y has been introduced to simplify the formulae.

A numerical example will be added, but only to illustrate orders of magnitude. Empirical research must be undertaken in order to verify the model and to obtain a better basis for further work. This is underway but must be postponed to later occasions. It is perfectly possible that the dependence of welfare on the armament components is different from the relations chosen. Our Model C only constitutes a first orientation about the type of research needed.

The real incomes expressed in US dollars (1980) are of the order of magnitude of 2500 for x_1 and 1250 for x_2. The values chosen for the αs and the βs are:

$$\alpha_{11} = 0.06 \quad \alpha_{12} = 0.05 \quad \alpha_{21} = 0.05 \quad \alpha_{22} = 0.07 \quad (4.13)$$
$$\beta_{11} = 0.015 \quad \beta_{12} = 0.015 \quad \beta_{21} = 0.03 \quad \beta_{22} = 0.03 \quad (4.14)$$

These figures satisfy some conditions we considered imperative, namely:

(i) $\alpha_{21} < \alpha_{11}$; $\alpha_{12} < \alpha_{22}$ (cf. Equations (4.7) and (4.9));

(ii) all βs are considerably smaller than the αs, expressing the fact that today both superpowers have much more offensive than defensive weapons.

(iii) $\alpha_{12} = \alpha_{21}$, expressing that the damage to be expected from a unit of offensive weapons is roughly equal in both directions; and

(iv) the SU coefficients are roughly twice the US coefficients, since $x_2 = \dfrac{1}{2} x_1$; but it remains unclear whether, for the offensive weapons, this should apply to α_{22} versus α_{11} or to $\alpha_{22} - \alpha_{12}$ versus $\alpha_{11} - \alpha_{21}$, as we did. This is the issue most in need of further research.

With the coefficients (4.13) and (4.14) the following solutions were obtained (Tables 4.1 and 4.2).

Table 4.1 Solutions of the unknowns (rounded)

	y_1	y_2	a_1	a_2	b_1	b_2	ω_1	ω_2	$\Omega = \omega_1 + \omega_2$
Problem I	2327	1077	139	139	34	34	7.91	7.30	15.20
Problem I'	2388	1138	79	79	33	33	7.93	7.34	15.27
Problem II	2405	1137	17	34	79	79	7.58	7.85	15.43

Table 4.2 Armament expenditures as a percentage of national income

	1 (United States)			2 (Soviet Union)		
	Offensive	Defensive	Total	Offensive	Defensive	Total
Problem I	5.6	1.4	6.9	11.1	2.7	13.8
Problem I'	3.2	1.3	4.5	6.3	2.6	9.0
Problem II	0.7	3.2	3.8	2.7	6.3	9.0

It should be noted that in particular the figure for a_2 (offensive weapons of country 2) is very sensitive to the value chosen for α_{22}. The model setup implies the assumption that in Problem II the propensity to spend on arms depends on y and that implies that transfers v_2 would be spent partly on arms. In this respect the model needs revision. This appears to hit on difficulties we have not solved so far and their treatment was postponed to later. The model is meant as an illustration. For the situation described in Problem I, where country 1 maximises utility, the figures in Table 4.2 for total armament expenditures are very close to reality in 1985/86.

4.9   THE LIMITS OF SOVEREIGN POLICIES

The results of the integration approach can be expected to be similar to the results of the separate welfare and security approaches, namely that sovereign policies fail to produce an optimal level of welfare-cum-security, as soon as external effects occur. For welfare environmental aspects show such effects and for security such effects are characteristic.

This has been shown by various authors as well as by the models we ourselves constructed.

We saw that in Model A, Problem II, all the resources available are devoted to the civilian economy, allowing it to grow at the maximum feasible rate, without diverting any resources to the production of arms. This is naturally to be expected, when the negative effect of armaments on the security of the other country is directly taken into account in decision-making. Today we observe that provinces within one sovereign country do not arm against one another. This is a strong argument in favour of taking decisions about armament and security at the world level.

In Problem I, where the two countries do not coordinate their activities but act at cross-purposes, taking only their own shortsighted interests into account, they can end up hurting themselves, if they burden their economies with mutual arms expenditures. However, in this model, it is found that if the arms are sufficiently defensive, the two countries spend nothing for arms:

If $e = c/bd > 1$, $\mu_1 = \mu_2 = 0$,

i.e. no resources are allocated to the military sector. This is the case if c, the internal gain in security from the production of arms, is large compared to d, the external loss of security (i.e.

if the arms are predominantly defensive) and/or the potential growth factor b of the civilian economy is small, so that the economy is unable to sustain an extensive arms industry.

With more highly offensive arms, or a higher potential growth factor,

if $e = c/bd < 1$, $\mu_1 = \mu_2 = 1 - e = 1 - c/bd$,

i.e. the fraction of resources spent on arms is the higher, the more offensive the arms are, and the more productive the civilian economy. The actual growth factor of the economy,

$g = b(1 - \mu_1) = be = c/d$

is the lower, the more offensive the arms are. If $c < d$, i.e. the external loss of security exceeds the internal gain, then the growth factor is less than 1, and the economies of the two countries are contracting over time, as a consequence of heavy arms expenditures.

How do countries choose between more or less offensive military technologies, if they do not coordinate their decisions? A country that is only interested in maintaining its own security, without deliberately aiming at reducing the security of the other country, will choose the military technology that gives it the highest amount of internal security per unit of resources spent, without taking into consideration the loss of security caused for the other country. Therefore, if one country discovers a new weapons technology which is inexpensive and highly defensive, it will be in its interest to make that technology available to the other country, out of self-interest. That can induce the other country to shift to a more defensive and less threatening form of arms production. Arthur Cox (1981), for example, has argued that it would be in the interest of the United States to make its most reliable computers available to the Soviet Union for its anti-missile warning system, so that the Soviet Union would not launch a retaliatory strike because of computer error.

Some typical examples of defensive conventional arms are barriers against tanks in fixed positions, land mines, anti-tank and anti-aircraft weapons, and shore batteries in fixed emplacements. They can be used to repel aggression, but cannot be used to carry out aggression.

Some typical conventional offensive arms are tanks, especially when accompanied by fuel tanks for advances over a great distance, bombers, landing craft and aircraft carriers. These weapons can be used for military operations far beyond a country's home territory.

By simultaneously improving its defence capabilities and

deliberately reducing its offensive forces, a country can increase its own security against attacks and also reduce the fear of adversaries of being attacked. Such a unilateral shift, which is neither armament nor disarmament, but can be called *trans*armament, enables a country to reduce the danger of war, without risk to its own security. On the contrary, it will increase its own security, as well as the security of other countries.

It is obvious that negotiations for mutual disarmament and for joint measures to reduce the danger of war should be pursued rigorously. But negotiations should never be used as an excuse for not undertaking unilateral steps that can help reduce the danger of war, without a risk to a country's own security. Transarmament from offensive to defensive arms is one such step.

Is the Strategic Defence Initiative (SDI) a defensive system? By itself, it would not pose a threat to anyone, and would be purely defensive, although it is doubtful how effective a defence against nuclear weapons could ever be. Current plans only foresee a defence against ballistic missiles that leave the atmosphere, not against cruise missiles or even nuclear weapons smuggled by terrorists. However, the fact that it may turn out not to be feasible to develop a reliable defensive system would be no reason not to try. But when a defensive system against missiles is combined with nuclear missiles, the combination of the two yields a highly *offensive* system. Without a defence, no sane leader would ever want to launch nuclear missiles, out of fear of retaliation. But with a defensive shield against retaliation, a first strike, or at least the threat of a first strike to win concessions, might become conceivable in the mind of a totally ruthless national leader.

Another problem with the proposed system of space-based lasers is that those laser beams could not only be aimed at an opponent's missiles, but also at its space stations. Whoever fired these laser beams first could wipe out the space stations of an opponent. Whoever hesitated during a crisis would risk losing his space stations. This would introduce a new source of crisis instability.

Furthermore, these space stations would have to react so quickly that human control would have to be eliminated, leaving decisions to pre-programmed computers. Do we want to risk the outbreak of a world war due to a computer error?

For these and other reasons, SDI does not appear to offer a solution to the threat of nuclear war. The solution will more likely have to be found in the political rather than the purely technical domain.

The results obtained with Model C in section 4.8 can be interpreted as follows. Equation (4.12) shows that significant non-military security expenditures are part of the optimum: no less than half of the difference in national expenditures should be transferred from nation 1 to nation 2.

For the military expenditures we can derive from (4.1) to (4.10): the relative importance of defensive to offensive weapons has to be changed in favour of defensive weapons, that is *transarmament* is highly desirable.

From the numerical example summarised in Table 4.1 we see that a considerable reduction in offensive armament expenditure characterises the solution of Problem II, that is, an attempt to cooperate or to shift to a supranational way of decision-making. Our findings are an encouragement to extensive further empirical work and to speed up negotiations on a common policy of security.

REFERENCES

Adler Karlsson, G. (1967), *Funktionssocialism*, Oskarhamn, Bokförlaget Prisma (Swedish; also available in English).

Baer-Kaupert, F.-W. (1985), 'Peace and the Nuclear Paradox', *NATO Review*, April, pp. 17–23 (adapted from Europa-Archiv, Bonn).

Ball, R.J. (ed.) (1973), *The International Linkage of National Economic Models*, Amsterdam, North-Holland.

Cox, Arthur (1981), *Russian Roulette: The Superpower Game*, New York, Times Books.

Deutsch, K.W. (1984), 'Zur Bedeutung von Weltmodellen — Verstehen lernen, wie sich die Welt verändert', *W.Z.B.-Mitteilungen* No. 25, September, pp. 12–15.

Fischer, D. (1977), 'Externalities and interdependence in a Von Neumann Growth Model', in R. Henn and O. Moeschlin (eds), *Mathematical Economics and Game Theory: Essays in Honor of Oskar Morgenstern*, New York, Springer Verlag.

Kornai, J. (1971), *Rush versus Harmonic Growth*, Amsterdam, North-Holland.

Morgenstern, O. and G.L. Thompson (1976), *Mathematical Theory of Expanding and Contracting Economies*, Lexington, MA, Lexington Books.

Palme, O. (1982), Chairman, Independent Commission on Disarmament and Security Issues, *Common Security*, New York, Simon and Schuster.

Spoor, A. (1985), 'Defensieschild alleen samen met Russen acceptabel', (Dutch; Defence shield only acceptable together with Russians), *NRC/Handelsblad*, 11 February, p. 8.

Tinbergen, J. (1964), *Central Planning*, New Haven and London, Yale University Press.

—— (1984), 'On collective and part-collective goods', *De Economist* 132, pp. 171–82.

—— (1985), *Production, Income and Welfare*, Brighton, Wheatsheaf Books, Ch. 5.

UNCTAD (1985), 'International Commodity Agreements', *UNCTAD Bulletin*, June/July, pp. 3–6.

Waelbroeck, J.L. (1976), *The Models of Project Link*, Amsterdam, North-Holland.

Wiles, P. (1978), 'Our shaky data base', in W. Krelle and A. F. Shorroks (eds), *Personal Income Distribution*, Amsterdam, New York, Oxford, North-Holland Publ. Comp.

5 Spatial Aspects of the Optimum Order

5.1 INTRODUCTION

So far we have neglected the spatial dimensions. Humankind lives in *three-dimensional space* and the concepts and institutions discussed in earlier chapters may vary spatially. It is not only natural phenomena that vary in space (e.g. temperature) but also economic variables may be different in different *locations*. Wheat production occurs close to the earth's surface and is possible only in limited areas of the earth's surface. Human beings live in cities, in villages or in isolation. Location also introduces the concept of *transportation* from one location to another, and *communication* between different locations. The spatial element considerably complicates society and its institutions, and a number of these complications will be discussed in this chapter. In the real world there are very few nations where space and distance play a subordinate role—for instance, Hong Kong or Gibraltar. Space and distance play a relatively minor role in small countries such as the Caribbean islands, Andorra or Luxembourg and even in the Netherlands or Belgium location and distance play minor roles in comparison to the Soviet Union or the United States, or in an activity like sea transport. In the present chapter the impact on our subject as a consequence of space will be discussed.

5.2 THE VERTICAL DIMENSION

Of the three dimensions in which we live, the *vertical* is the most peculiar, partly as a consequence of gravity. Whereas our ordinary life takes place in close proximity to the earth's surface, sinking a mine gives us access to coal or mineral ores, both materials of great importance. Downward exploration into the earth can also give access to water, a matter of immense importance in arid regions. The water may also be forced upward under pressure as in the geysers of Iceland. Under the seas— which cover about three-quarters of the earth's surface—fish are hunted by fishermen; fish may also be 'harvested' on fish farms and so may oysters and other molluscs. Finally, below the seabed we now drill for oil and we have just started to collect manganese nodules from the bottom of the deep seas—possibly a promising new industry (cf. Mann Borgese, 1985).

So much for downward exploration. We have also learned to move upward, at present mainly by aircraft, and the atmosphere is the environment of a flourishing transportation industry for human beings and products.

Earlier we had learned to project objects through the atmosphere describing *ballistic paths*; starting with stones and followed by increasingly lethal objects. Using stronger firepower (gunpowder, dynamite and other explosives, and now nuclear energy) movements other than from earth to earth became possible. We are now able to put *satellites* in an orbit around the earth for both peaceful and offensive purposes. Finally, with the application of still more energy we have succeeded in launching scientific instruments into outer space to observe other planets. Astronauts have even landed on the moon. A directly empirical branch of astronomy was thus added to the existing branches. Some enthusiasts dream of visiting other planetary systems; but we have to keep in mind that even at the speed of light (300,000 km/sec) it takes five years to reach the nearest star.

Unfortunately, as already mentioned, most of the movements in outer space are devoted to military purposes. We shall deal with these when discussing security issues.

In comparison to the vertical movements described above some modest additional vertical movements are those necessary or desirable in mountainous countries. Switzerland is the obvious European example of course, but each continent has its mountain ranges. Civil engineering and transportation systems have developed impressive technologies, especially for recreational purposes. Similar activities are involved in skyscraper construction, with the United States as the pioneer.

5.3   THE HORIZONTAL DIMENSIONS: GEOGRAPHICAL ASPECTS OF SOCIETY

The other two dimensions which are the basis for geography and the larger part of the socio-economic and security activities occur in a plane that may be described by two coordinates: latitude and longitude. The earth's surface is similar to that of a globe, and cannot be exactly reproduced on a plane. We mentioned earlier that only one quarter of the surface is land. The land surface is divided into more than 150 *sovereign nations*, which have appropriated part of the adjacent sea area, the so-called *exclusive economic zone* (EEZ). There are enormous differences in size and economic importance between the nations. In population the largest, China, is about a million times that of some of the smallest. Consumption per capita varies between the larger ones in a ratio of about 1 (India) to 17 (US) (cf. Kravis *et al.*, 1982). Production of all kinds of goods and services varies as a consequence of differences in mineral deposits, climates, fertility of arable land and skills and preferences of the population. The consumption mix may be very different from the production mix. The differences are bridged by *international trade* or, for large countries, *inter-regional trade*. About half of the goods and services produced in one country (measured in terms of money value) cannot be transported (and hence traded). These are called *non-tradeables* and consist of buildings and their uses, many consumer services (hair-dressing, retail trade services) and cultural activities: primary and secondary education, government services. The other half of production may be—but is not necessarily—traded: large countries' international trade is less than one-half of GNP. Upon some assumptions *free international trade* is part of the optimum economic order.

The introduction of a geographical or locational dimension to economic variables means that an additional index is needed to describe an economy's elements. Production must not only be characterised by the types of good, but also by its location. We only have a one-dimensional list (or vector) if we consider the sorts of good; it becomes a two-dimensional table (or matrix) if we add the location index. This matrix may show, in one column total, the total production of a *branch of industry*, and by one row total, the total production of a geographical area (*region*). Both totals have to satisfy certain conditions. Branch totals have to correspond to the total numbers of workers of various types, with the demand for the branch's products, etc. Regional totals have to satisfy certain relations with the region's total population, for instance. It is possible to organise planning and management of production in two ways: either branch by branch or region by region. Soviet planning experimented with both and finally settled on the branch by branch approach.

Often each member of the managing board of a large corporation deals with one product and with one local unit. This also constitutes the matrix approach.

An interesting additional aspect of the spatial side of an optimal socio-economic order is the distribution of the population over towns and villages of different size and the location of these centres. Centres are agglomerations of production units (factories, schools) of a long list of products each with optimal sizes. These sizes depend on the total costs of production and distribution to the consumer. Villages are small agglomerations built around, perhaps, one bakery, whereas large cities may be agglomerations around a steel-producing and processing complex, with all sorts of typical industries as the possible development 'poles' in between. Recently a considerable amount of research has been devoted to these problems (cf. Bos, 1964; Klaassen *et al.*, 1981; Despontin *et al.*, 1984; Paelinck, 1985).

Because of the lifespan of buildings considerable time-lags may exist between the factors at work and the result of dispersion. Most countries can only partially optimise the location of the *additional production and population*. In rare cases, newly recovered land can be designed optimally. A micro-example is the physical planning of newly recovered land in the Netherlands. A somewhat more macro-physical plan may accompany the construction of a new capital (e.g. Brasilia, Islamabad).

5.4 OPTIMAL LEVELS OF DECISION-MAKING

We stated earlier that the world economy and society consist of more than 150 sovereign nation-states of very different sizes and per capita consumption. Obviously, this state of affairs—in many respects bizarre, if not grotesque—is the outcome of history, and the historical process is composed of a great many unrelated, almost random elements. This is a very appropriate stage at which to specify the main question dealt with in this book. Is the way the world is managed near an optimum; has *laisser-faire* worked optimally? Can we design an optimal way of managing world society? Clearly economic science, and more particularly *business economics* (German: *Betriebswirtschaftslehre*) is able to make a significant contribution. We shall elaborate on what we found with the aid of Model C, in sections 4.8 and 4.9, and generalise some of these findings.

In order to operate the world economy (taken in our generalised sense) its citizens have to make a very large number of decisions, day after day, week after week, and so on. A number of decisions are made by individuals, but the more important ones are made by groups of individuals. There are many sorts of group and a considerable number of them are part of larger bodies organised as *hierarchies*. This applies to single enterprises, but also to large integrated enterprises such as multinationals. There is also a hierarchy of governmental authorities in each nation and there are a few supranational hierarchies, for instance the Coal and Steel Community within the European Community.

Upon closer analysis two questions arise almost automatically. The first is, which is the most appropriate group of decision-makers to decide on a given question or problem to be solved? This question takes for granted the existence of all necessary groups. The second question is whether new groups should be established in order to solve a given set of problems in the best way (optimally). Since the main emphasis in our analysis is on governmental decisions we assume that a hierarchical structure of relevant decision-making groups is necessary. This implies that we can use the concept of level instead of group, since a hierarchy orders the groups at successive levels. In government structures levels are usually related to geographical areas: a nation-state with a national government is composed of provinces with provincial governments; each province is subdivided into municipalities with municipal governments. A higher level then automatically means a larger territory with its population; its representative body or parliament represents the interests of a larger population.

Our first question now becomes: which government level is the optimal level to solve a given problem? Our answer is twofold: (i) the optimal level is the lowest possible level in order that a maximum of participation and a maximum of information be used; and (ii) the level is high enough to entail negligible external effects. By external effects we mean effects on the welfare of individuals living outside the area for which the decision-makers are responsible. Decisions affecting only the local population, for instance, should be made at the municipal level. Decisions affecting inhabitants of all or some provinces should be made at the national level. Decisions to prevent acid rain should probably be taken at the international level. Such authorities may not yet exist, or not have the competence to decide, or not have the power to implement their decisions. Obviously *decisions on security cannot be optimal when made by sovereign nations* as we found in sections 4.8 and 4.9 for Model C.

The second question now applies: authorities needed for optimal solutions to important problems—world security being one—may not exist but have to be created. We shall find that a number of supranational authorities which are badly needed do not yet exist; their creation appears to be urgent.

It is not only authorities at higher levels than those in existence that are lacking, but also at other levels. Management science provides us with some criteria to judge the efficiency of a given hierarchical system. For a hierarchy to be efficient each member at a higher level has to control a number of members at the next lower level. The number which can effectively be controlled by one supervisor is called the *span of control* and usually is of the order of 5–10. It depends, of course, on the nature of the problems to be solved.

With regard to the main problem of Part I of this book—the optimal institutional setup to maximise world welfare-cum-security—we conclude that decisions must be made at a level encompassing at least the two superpowers, and preferably the world at large. Only then will common security be attained.

In Chapters 7 and 11 we shall evaluate in more detail the present system of world management and propose a better structure. Our starting point will be that a General Assembly of over 150 members cannot be a level of decision-making of any use to an optimal management of our planet.

We mentioned also that the subdivision into geographical units of a given area raises questions of optimality. In a hierarchy one aspect that can be chosen is the span of control. There are more criteria for an optimal subdivision: for example, homogeneity in several respects—natural resources, language, history and other cultural characteristics. In an attempt to find the optimal management structure for the world at large, we submit that in contrast to the existing subdivision into more than 150 sovereign nations some twelve to fifteen regional federations of comparable size should be the building-blocks. Some of the most important existing large powers should be among them: China, the Soviet Union, the USA and India, for instance. Another unit might be the European Community. Other potential 'building-blocks' and some related questions will be taken up in Chapter 11.

5.5   SOME OTHER EXAMPLES OF THE NEED FOR SUPRA-NATIONAL DECISION-MAKING

Returning to the spatial aspects of the optimal order we should mention some additional problems whose solution requires decisions at higher than national levels. In passing we have already mentioned environmental problems. Most require decisions at a continental level, and some even at the world level.

In a report to the Club of Rome, *Reshaping the International Order* (RIO), a group presided over by J. Tinbergen (Tinbergen *et al.*, 1976), a number of activities are dealt with whose optimal extent and distribution can be attained by cooperation at the world level. Such cooperation is a weak form of decision-making and so the activities treated are part of this section's subject. They are (in addition to those already treated): running the monetary system, development finance, food production and distribution, industrialisation and international trade, supply of energy and minerals, research and technological development, supervising transnational enterprises. Ocean management has also been dealt with in RIO and will be discussed separately in section 5.7, since it combines all three spatial aspects and, moreover, constitutes the most advanced of all themes concerned.

For each of the activities listed institutions exist whose tasks are related. Thus, the International Monetary Fund (IMF) plays an important role in the world's monetary systems. The World Bank Group, composed of the World Bank (International Bank for Reconstruction and Development), the International Finance Corporation and the International Development Association, plays an important role in co-financing, in different ways, the investments needed for economic development. Food production and distribution are furthered by the UN Food and Agricultural Organisation (FAO) and the International Fund for Agricultural Development (IFAD). Industrialisation of developing countries is supported by the United Nations Industrial Development Organisation (UNIDO). International trade is the area of responsibility of the United Nations Conference on Trade and Development (UNCTAD), whereas negotiations on and supervision of the impediments to international trade are organised by the General Agreement on Tariffs and Trade (GATT).

This list is not comprehensive. The common feature of all these institutions is that they do not have the competence and power needed to constitute, as a set of institutions, an optimal world order to manage our planet. They are, in many cases, a beginning and their competences have developed; but this development is often blocked by powerful establishments whose interests conflict. They are blocked by powerful nations or by transnational enterprises which are, in the present international structure, privileged and want to keep their privileges. This is understandable, but not acceptable to those who want the interests of world population as a whole to be protected. A complication of this conflict of interests is that often the interested groups are better informed about the technical details of the activities concerned. Improvement of the information flows towards interested groups may help to improve mutual understanding as well as the world management structure.

5.6 REGIONAL INTEGRATION

In section 5.3 we pointed out the (at least) two-dimensional character of economies or societies if both the sort of product or activity and its geographical location are to be described. Consequently there is also a choice between planning or managing the total economy in two different ways: (1) managing it as a set of industries with different products; and (2) managing it as a set of geographical units. In the optimal order a two-fold harmony must exist: the relative importance of the industries must match the composition of demand; and the relative importance of the geographical units must match the criteria listed at the end of section 5.4 (span of control, homogeneity with regard to natural resources, cultural aspects, etc.).

Geographical or regional integration is particularly important for security. Experience shows that armed conflicts between the geographical regions of an integrated area are considerably less likely than they were before integration. Integration usually implies the creation of institutions for the solution of conflicts by legal means. Armed conflicts between the provinces of the Netherlands ceased after the Republic of the United Provinces (the Union) was established. Armed conflicts between German states ceased after the establishment of the Reich in 1871. After the civil war, the United States of America changed their ineffective federation into a real federation and no war between states has taken place. The point is that integration almost automatically implies the creation of institutions for conflict resolution among the constituent parts of the integrated territory.

Regional integration also constitutes a system for creating the non-existent but desirable levels of decision-making discussed in section 5.4, and to be resumed in Chapter 11.

5.7   USE OF THE SEAS

In section 5.2, dealing with the vertical dimension of human environment, the seas were mentioned briefly and in section 5.3, dealing with the horizontal, 'geographical' dimensions, we reminded the reader of the large area of the earth covered by oceans and seas. In addition to these important spatial aspects the seas deserve our special attention because of their being the subject of the most advanced ideas about global management already formulated in a new draft Law of the Sea (LoS), attained over a period of nine years of negotiations. These negotiations took place in the Conference on the LoS, convened by the UN General Assembly of 1973. The origin of this greatest accomplishment of the United Nations is the 'historic three-hour address delivered by Dr Arvid Pardo, ambassador of Malta, before the General Assembly of the United Nations on November 1, 1967'—to quote Professor Elisabeth Mann Borgese (1985, p. 135). In this address the concept of 'common heritage of mankind' was introduced, meaning that the seas outside the exclusive economic zone (EEZ) could not be appropriated by any nation, individual or company; and that all the riches in and below the seas should be managed for the benefit of the world population. In addition they should be managed for peaceful purposes, keeping in mind the interests of future generations. This latter aspect will be discussed in Chapter 6, where the time dimension of the optimal socio-economic order is discussed.

In comparison to the main elements of the law of the sea for centuries, free navigation outside the territorial seas (only three miles wide) and conditions of passage through straits, the problems now faced by a proper management of the world's oceans and seas are numerous and complicated. Shipping uses increasingly large vessels including oil tankers which increase the danger of pollution of the seas and coasts in the event of spillages. Fishing has increased to such an extent as to lead to overfishing, threatening the extinction of some species, for instance whales.

Mining is a new activity, first of mineral oil in the seas above the continental shelves, where the seas were claimed by the coastal states and divided by lines at equal distances from the (rectified) coastal lines. Mining has now become possible in the deepest parts of the oceans, in particular in the form of 'catching' nodules containing manganese, nickel, copper and cobalt. Elisabeth Mann Borgese (1985, p. 74) claims that at the time of writing nodules have to contain at least 27 per cent of manganese, 1.5 per cent of nickel, 1.3 per cent of copper and 0.24 per cent of cobalt to be cost-effective.

The outcome of nine years of negotiation was a draft convention in which the management of these many activities was set out. In April 1982 it was approved by 130 nations in favour (with 4 against and 17 abstaining). By 1985 143 nations had signed the convention. Those nations which oppose the convention have the technical know-how to undertake deep-sea mining and hence prefer not to adhere to the principle of a common heritage; some or all of the 17 abstaining nations may be in a similar position. This attitude reflects the political shift to the Right in several industrial countries. We must hope that nevertheless the LoS Convention will be ratified by a sufficient number of governments, in the interest of the world at large. Fifty are needed.

The main new institutions the Draft Convention creates are an International Seabed Authority, with an Assembly setting the general policy, an Executive Council with Specialised Commissions and a Secretariat. In addition an operational arm, The Enterprise, to organise joint ventures with private enterprises, bringing in the technological know-how. Out of the profits, funding for research, conservation of the ocean environment and for development purposes can be made, all of them serving the interests of the world at large. Much will depend on the effectiveness of the newly created institutions. First-rate managers will be needed with a broad vision. A general system for the peaceful settlement of disputes completes the institutional setup.

At the time of writing the Preparatory Commission for the International Seabed Authority and the International Tribunal and one Special Commission are able to undertake activities while waiting for the necessary number of ratifications. During its second session the Preparatory Commission received a proposal from Austria to establish, under its auspices, a Joint Enterprise for Exploration, Research and Development (JEFERAD). In Professor Mann Borgese's view this is the

only way for the Preparatory Commission to discharge its
responsibilities to take all necessary steps for the early entry into
effective operation of the Enterprise (cf. Mann Borgese, 1985a).

5.8   USE OF THE ATMOSPHERE AND OUTER SPACE

There is no clearly demarcated frontier between earth's atmosphere and outer space. Aviation is among the initial activities
using the atmosphere. They are supervised by the specialised
agency of the United Nations International Civil Aviation
Organisation (ICAO). One of the problems ICAO had to face
in 1977 was the security of air travel, in particular the protection
of passengers and crews against hijacking. The way this problem
was dealt with is described in some detail by Kaufmann (1980,
pp. 154–8) as an 'example of optimalised decision-making'.

In addition to civil aviation, intensive use has also been made
of the atmosphere by military purposes especially in World War
II and since then in local wars, but also for 'reconnaissance'
(also called 'espionage') purposes in peacetime. The atmosphere
was also used for centuries by all forms of firearms (ballistic
use).

More recently the atmosphere and outer space have been used
by satellites, the first example being the launching of the Soviet
Sputnik (1957). At present satellites are used for various peaceful
purposes such as meteorological and communication (TV programmes), and astronomical and related research, as set out in
section 5.2.

Similar to the new LoS, the use of the atmosphere and
outer space (together to be called simply 'space') the optimal
management had best be entrusted to an institution representing
the world population as a whole and be considered as the
heritage of mankind.

REFERENCES

Bos, H.C. (1964), *Spatial Dispersion of Economic Activity*, Rotterdam,
    Rotterdam University Press.
Despontin, M., Nijkamp, P. and Spronk, J. (eds) (1984), *Macro-economic
    planning with conflicting goals*, Berlin, Heidelberg, New York and Tokyo,
    Springer Verlag.
Kaufmann, J. (1980), *United Nations Decision-Making*, Alphen aan den Rijn

and Rockville MD, USA, Sijthoff and Noordhoff.

Klaassen, L.H., Molle, W.T.M. and Paelinck, J.H.P. (eds) (1981), *Dynamics of Urban Development*, Aldershot, Gower.

Kravis, I.B., Heston, A. and Summers, R. (1982), *World Product and Income*, Baltimore and London, The Johns Hopkins Press (for the World Bank).

Mann Borgese, E. (1985), *The Mines of Neptune*, New York, Abrams.

—— (1985a), 'What can developing countries gain from the UN Convention on the Law of the Sea?', *Trade and Development*, pp. 123–30, New York, United Nations.

Paelinck, J.H.P. *et al.* (1985), *Eléments d'analyse économique spatiale*, Paris, Editions Anthropos.

Tinbergen, J. *et al.* (1976), *Reshaping the International Order*, New York, E.P. Dutton.

6 Time Aspects of the Optimum Order

6.1 THE NATURE OF TIME; TYPES OF MOVEMENT

Before Einstein's theory of relativity, space and time were considered to be mutually independent coordinates. The world of human history was four-dimensional, but all points in space were thought to show, on their astronomical clocks, the same time. (Societies' clocks show different times for practical purposes of daily life: they have to indicate 12 o'clock when the sun is at its highest position.)

In the theory of relativity astronomical time is no longer the same everywhere: it depends on the velocity with which an object is moving. For practical purposes we can use the pre-Einsteinian view, however, since the time deviations are negligible as long as the velocity of the object's movement is negligible in comparison to the velocity of light.

Changes of a variable's value or location in the course of time are called *movements* and the present chapter will deal with movements of all variables relevant to the optimum order. Before specifying which variable we consider relevant two general observations will be made. First, the distinction between two types of movement: trends or *one-sided* movements are those where the figure indicating a value or a location is either rising all the time or falling, with the limiting case of no movement or constancy. *Cyclical* movements are successions of upward and downward movements, whether regular (like a sine curve) or irregular, as is much more often the case in economic history. Second, the cause or causes of the movement of a variable. Here we make a distinction between *exogenous* and *endogenous* causes or explanations of an observed or an anticipated movement. If a variable of an economy is moving because it is linked to a variable outside that economy we speak of an exogenous causation or explanation. A simple example is a movement linked to the environment's temperature, or another climatic phenomenon (sunshine, rainfall, etc.). Recently the climate is beginning to be influenced by human activities, however. (In section 6.2 more examples will be discussed.) An endogenous movement of an economy's variable is one caused by or linked to the movement of other variables of that economy. One example is movements in wage rates and price levels. Another example is the price of pork and the supply of pork. For a long time both moved in cycles: a year and a half after a relatively high price supply is relatively high. On the pork market this high supply can only be sold if the price falls. This leads to a relatively low supply a year and a half later, and so on. In contradistinction to price cycles caused by seasonal variations the pork cycle finds its origin in a mechanism internal to the economy.

6.2 ESSENTIAL EXTERNAL CAUSES OF ECONOMIC MOVEMENTS

In this section the most important external variables to which economic variables are linked will be discussed. One set of such variables are *climatological*. We have already mentioned temperature, sunshine and rainfall. These variables change over time and are important determinants of agricultural production. For all types of agricultural products the growth process is affected by climatic variables at each phase in their growth. Storms, hail or hurricanes may exert strongly negative influences. Some of these effects can be controlled up to a point by protective strategies, such as the use of glasshouses or planting on the warm side of a mountain range.

A second set of external variables are *demographic*. The size and age composition of a nation's population and its ethnic composition affect a range of economic variables, such as labour supply and composition of the needs and desires and so part of the demand for all goods produced. The age composition is of particular importance to organising education. A further specification of the population's intellectual, physiological and psychological characteristics will enter the picture here.

A third set of external variables are *technological*. The full impact of this set can be seen in leading developed countries, but in most less developed countries too, a complex range of technological know-how is available and codetermines the mix

of production processes operating in each nation. Global technological knowledge is continually enriched by new discoveries and
inventions. Systematic activities directed at discovering new facts
or relationships are the task of laboratories; most of these are
attached to industries or universities. Obviously a considerable
role is played by good or bad luck. Educational institutions have
the dual task of singling out talented individuals to advance the
search for knowledge. In addition to the general stock of
knowledge a nation's technological force also depends on the
skills of all individual workers developed at school and, later,
on the job.

A fourth set of external variables significant to an economy
(or to the joint economies of the world) consists of the *stocks
of resources*, living and dead, from the world's fauna and flora
and its reserves of minerals in the widest sense, especially
energetic and metal ores. Some resources are *inexhaustible*: those
derived from solar radiation and from human inventiveness;
others are *exhaustible*, quickly or slowly. Quickly exhaustible
resources are fuels of many kinds because they can be used once
only; this applies to coal, oil and gas. Slowly exhaustible are the
stocks of metals which are not consumed but used in the restricted
sense. They can be recovered after the object made from them
has become obsolete. In the recovery process a small part is
scattered in space and lost. With the aid of new technology we
can, however, increase the quantity of satisfaction or *welfare*
derived from one unit of resources. We can invent lighter
structures or more efficient machines; we can save on the use
of energy; and so on.

As a fifth set of external variables we shall introduce a set
which is considered to be external in traditional economics, but
not in our generalised economics and we call it *international
politics*—the possible source of conflicts between nations whose
settlement was, in the past, considered the justification of war.

6.3   MAIN SOCIO-ECONOMIC VARIABLES TO BE
PLANNED OR ANTICIPATED

Movement over time of the economy (or economies) considered
will be described by a number of variables characterising the
main features of these economies. A general impression may be
obtained by a macro-model and the variables appearing in it.
These variables will be important to all countries. Micro-models

and their variables will differ much more and reflect each country's specialities. We restrict ourselves to a list of macro-variables.

Population, subdivided into age groups, is fundamental. The age groups can be classified as (i) young people, not yet available for participation in the production process; (ii) people available for employment in the process of production or education; and (iii) people no longer assumed to be gainfully employed.

Employment, working time and *productivity*, apply to the second age group, whose multiplication yields total *production volume*. This constitutes the sum total of *consumption, investment* and *export surplus*; the latter being *exports* minus *imports* of goods and services.

Productivity is highly dependent on the total capital stock; this consists of physical and human capital (i.e. capital invested in the education of the population).

Both consumption and investment can be subdivided into private or individual, and collective consumption or investment; the latter two further subdivided into a civilian and a military component.

So far all concepts have been defined in physical terms. Multiplying them by their *prices* (for goods and services) and *wage rates* (for employment) yields their *money value*. Prices may be *market* prices or *factor cost* prices, in which indirect taxes (minus subsidies) are not included.

6.4 ELEMENTS OF OPTIMALITY IN DEVELOPMENT: WHOSE UTILITY?

Of all the aspects of an optimal order treated in Chapters 4, 5 and 6 the time dimension contains difficulties known from what in all economic problems distinguishes dynamics from statics. In the present section some of these difficulties will be set out and discussed without making an attempt to conclude with one definition of optimal development. The most important authors who have dealt with the subject have not reached a common point of view—the situation we also found when we considered the timeless and spaceless order, discussed in Chapter 4 (cf. Koopmans, 1976).

Obviously optimality always means that some sort of utility or welfare per person has to be maximised, but on closer consideration some questions arise. First, whose utility? Inagaki (1970) rightly criticises theories that implicitly assume the economy for which future development must be planned to be a 'society of immortals'. Human beings have a finite life and in any given time unit only those alive can make decisions. There exists some form of common decision-making with regard to development planning, and Inagaki indicates the result as instantaneous government (IG) making the relevant decisions. This brief summary conceals a host of unspecified details. In a centrally planned economy the government chooses from a number of alternative plans constructed by a central planning agency, possibly based on directives from that government and after amendments of the chosen plan. In market economies the key variable for development—total net investment—is the total of an immense number of decisions by business executives, from big corporation executives to heads of one-man firms and executives of public corporations. A government exists, whose election may be the result of a parliamentary democracy, of which various types exist, but there are and have been other ways of government formation. In a market economy, or a mixed economy, the government only indirectly co-determines the volume of total investment, by the socio-economic policy it follows. This policy implies its total expenditure and the latter's distribution over the many categories of spending and the way this expenditure is financed. Part of the financing will be done through taxes of different kinds; part by loans.

In one of these very different ways, then, the government will formulate policy, keeping in mind that its decision-making affects in very different ways the interests of citizens of different ages, of different incomes and with varying characteristics. The government will also feel responsible—as citizens do—for future generations. Again, many problems arise. What relative weight will be given to the estimated future welfare of citizens now living and of future generations? Will future generations be better or worse off? The answers partly depend on the future course of the external causes of development, listed in section 6.2; climatological, demographic, technological, exhaustible and non-exhaustible resources, and international policies. The government's decisions partly depend also on the size of future generations in comparison to today's population.

We took as the criterion for optimality welfare per capita considerations. This implies that we do not consider it appropriate to select as our criterion something like 'total' welfare—the total for all individuals. We think such a criterion is meaningless.

The preceding argument referred to *one country*. Since there are many countries, all supposed to determine their own future, the main subject of this book—how common welfare and security can be attained—will reoccur, with all its difficulties.

6.5   MAXIMISING WELFARE PER CAPITA OVER WHAT TIME PERIOD?

After identifying the population whose welfare has to be maximised, the question must be answered: Over what period should their welfare be maximised? That period is called the *horizon*; it characterises the period that interests the individuals concerned. People with a short horizon are shortsighted or myopic; people with a long horizon are farsighted. The main reason for myopia is the uncertainty of future circumstances. Clearly myopia has great disadvantages and may cause disasters that might otherwise have been avoided. Investors of all kinds tend to match their horizon with the anticipated *lifetime* of the objects in which they invest. Houses may be kept in good condition over centuries. Investment in human beings (education) aims at enabling the educated individual to be employed in an attractive job, and so the pupil's lifetime is at stake.

Horizons in business or military investment depend on the speed of scientific—and hence technological—development (as discussed in section 6.2). Topical examples are to be found in the discussions on President Reagan's Strategic Defence Initiative. Many experts agree that considerable time will be needed before defence technologies against a rocket attack will be developed. The views in favour of common security also make sense only for the long time needed to reduce mutual mistrust between the superpowers.

Literally, the assumption of a finite horizon means that an individual is fully interested in what happens during that finite period and then suddenly loses all interest. This can only be considered realistic if a sudden change takes place. Such a change may be the individual's death and the absence of other individuals who take the same interest; or it may be the exhaustion of a vital resource, available in a finite quantity.

The finite availability of a vital resource need not entail the exhaustion of that resource after a given time period. It is conceivable that technological development is such that for the maintenance of a given level of welfare a decreasing quantity of the resource is needed, and the rate of decrease is enough to produce the level of welfare over an infinite period. An example is a decrease according to a geometrical series.

In the absence of a sudden change a finite horizon is indeed unrealistic. This is avoided if a *discounting process* is added; the simplest form of which is the assumption that interest for consecutive time units diminishes by a constant factor. Such an assumption is mathematically convenient and even more so, in a number of cases, if simultaneously the horizon is assumed to be infinitely long. This approach made Inagaki characterise the development aimed at to be 'a society of immortals', as mentioned in section 6.4. The approach may be defended, however, as a method to take into account the welfare of *future generations*.

6.6 DISCOUNTING FUTURE WELFARE?

The third question about maximising welfare over time precisely is whether discounting future welfare is an attractive method. It correctly reflects human psychology in cases where individuals plan for their own future. But does it also reflect the way the community should plan for the future? In a way discounting future welfare constitutes a form of discrimination, or of myopia; and myopia in a number of cases definitely is a vice.

An opposing argument is that in a limited portion only of all conceivable possibilities can we solve our problem without discounting future welfare (cf. Gale, 1967). Welfare in all future years constitutes a series of figures, with an indefinitely large number of members. In order to find a maximum of total welfare, the sum of the series must be finite. (We cannot compare infinitely large sums.) A finite sum will only be attained if the successive terms become smaller and smaller. This means that a form of discounting is the precondition for the existence of an optimum, if we assume an infinitely long horizon.

Summarising sections 6.4—6.6, we reach the conclusion that an optimal development process over time cannot always be defined. We found four categories of situations where such a process can be defined: (1) if a vital resource is available in a finite quantity and after a finite period is exhausted; (2) if a technological development implies the possibility to spread the consumption of such a resource over an infinitely long period; (3) if welfare in consecutive time units is discounted; and (4) if a finite horizon is assumed irrespective of the exhaustion of a vital resource.

6.7 SOME FEATURES OF THE OPTIMUM DEVELOPMENT OVER TIME

In this section we shall complete the sketch of the likely shape of the time-path of the variables characterising the optimum socio-economic order in the general sense, that is, including security variables and the instrument variables. We cannot offer more than a sketch, as long as we do not specify a model, with the precision of our illustrative models A, B and C, and as long as the choices discussed in sections 6.5 and 6.6 have not been made.

Trend movements will occur in the population, technology and resource variables and, as a consequence, the socio-economic variables listed in section 6.3. Population will expand, for quite some time to come, in most parts of the world but great efforts must be made to reduce population increase and overall population. Technological capabilities will continue to rise and as a consequence the discovery of additional resources will continue, but the demand for resources will also rise and the result of these two tendencies can only be estimated after extensive studies, now underway. Switching to non-exhaustible resources as well as pollution abatement must be furthered. In large parts of the world education and research should be expanded. Education should match the needs for the type of labour required by technological development and the latter geared to the quality of the total labour force available as a consequence of past education and training of generations available for production. Working hours should be used as one of the instruments for absorbing into the production process all who want to be gainfully occupied.

Cyclical movements around these trends should as far as possible be eliminated. Such elimination signifies the avoidance of unnecessary adjustments to changes in quantities produced and consumed and prices, adjustments requiring labour and possibly also capital. For *endogenous* cyclical movements this is possible, in principle. This may be illustrated by the example of the pork cycle mentioned in section 6.1. Regular information about the trend component and the cyclical component in prices and quantities sold combined with counselling about production planning may contribute to the cycle's virtual elimination. In the case of coffee and rubber, where comparable but somewhat more complicated cycles have existed over a long time period, advice about the planting of new trees is an additional instrument of market regulation.

The ordinary business cycle or Juglar is supposed to be endogenous. After World War II, governments and public opinion were fully aware of the Great Depression of the 1930s and Keynes' views on how to avoid its repetition, namely to work with public finance deficits in times of a threatening depression. For about twenty years cyclical movements of this type were weak, partly as a consequence of Keynes' *General Theory*. Meanwhile economic structures changed, and became less flexible. New forms of disequilibria resulted, especially the phenomenon known as *stagflation*. Stagnation of production and employment was no longer accompanied by price and wage reductions, as in past business cycles, but by price and wage rises; hence inflation. Economists do not yet agree on how to prevent this new type of disequilibrium in future and at what level to decide. One point of agreement is that a sovereign policy is not possible even for middle-sized countries like France.

Exogenous cyclical movements cannot completely be eliminated. This may be illustrated by a closer look at some seasonal fluctuations. Seasonal changes in temperature and rainfall cannot be changed. The consequences are seasonal fluctuations in production of vegetables, fruits, eggs, poultry, etc. and these can only be counteracted in a few cases, for instance by heating and artificial light. Consumption and price cycles may be eliminated, however, by storage or by processing the product into a non-perishable form.

This also applies to fluctuations in annual harvests as a consequence of variations in weather conditions between successive years, variations which may be part of the explanation of the three-year cycles known as Kitchins. Here storage may be the instrument to even out a large part of the quasi-cycle. Partly private futures trade takes care of this form of stabilisation.

Another important example of cycles presumably of an exogenous character are the so-called Kondratiefs with a wave-length of some fifty years. In the course of time several hypotheses on their causes have been made. At present the scholars who have contributed most to their explanation tend to consider the most important cause to be a certain clustering of innovative technological inventions (cf. Freeman, 1982; Van Roon, 1982; Kleinknecht, 1984). It seems likely that an optimal social order will be affected by such clusters, whose origin presumably is to be found in the world of research and development. It is not inconceivable, however, that instruments will be developed to even out clustering and so contribute to smoother economic development.

REFERENCES

Freeman, Chr. (1982), *The Economics of Industrial Innovation*, London, Frances Pinter (1st edition, 1974, Penguin Economics).

Gale, D. (1967), 'On optimal development in a multisector economy', *Review of Economic Studies* 34, pp. 1–13.

Inagaki, M. (1970), *Optimal Economic Growth*, Amsterdam, North-Holland Publishing.

Kleinknecht, A. (1984), *Innovation Patterns in Crisis and Prosperity: Schumpeter's Long Cycle Reconsidered*, Dissertation, Free University, Amsterdam, and Macmillan, London, 1986.

Koopmans, T.C. (1976), 'Concepts of optimality and their uses', Nobel Memorial Lecture, 11 December 1975, *Les prix Nobel en 1975*.

Van Roon, G. Chairman (1982), *Cyclical Fluctuations: an Interdisciplinary Approach*, Eighth International Economic History Congress, Budapest; Free University, Amsterdam, Koningslaan 31–33, 1075 AB Amsterdam).

Part II
Policies to Attain the Optimum

7 Managing our Planet

7.1 SUBJECTS COVERED IN PART II

Having outlined, in Part I, the optimal social order designed for the ultimate aim of international economic and security policies, we shall now attempt to identify the policies needed to attain that order. This is a very ambitious project and we are aware that most readers and fellow economists will consider it to be over-ambitious. We almost feel that an excuse is called for. We admit that the goal we set ourselves is ambitious. Yet we feel that an overwhelming majority of our colleagues, of policy-makers and of world citizens are suffering from the opposite attitude: that is, setting too modest tasks—even with the best intentions. Let us forget about the many who want to take the soft option and only engage in debate with those who want to give meaning to life. Scholars usually try to add to knowledge and understanding in as reliable a way as possible. Politicians want to make a contribution to welfare of the group they represent—or the group they think to be most in need of a welfare increase. Both scholars and politicians motivated by serious intentions try to be well-informed on the world's situation, its prospects and the most relevant forces at work. As a matter of course they are deeply impressed by the complex picture, by the innumerable forces at work, by the myriad conflicts threatening the world. Aware of the limitations of what conscious action can do they are forced into modest endeavours. This leads to research programmes or political programmes directed at a nearby target. Since even the most important scientific institutes and the most powerful political parties and their factions are only a small part of all such institutions, their totality offers a composite of an almost unstructured set of thousands of programmes, threatened by unplanned collision, partly counteracting each other and hence reducing the effectiveness of the effort. In a way the desire to do a good job forces many scholars and policy-makers into some sort of shortsightedness, even when in other respects they express long-term views.

It is this state of affairs that creates the need for a small number of both professions—scientists and politicians—who dare to stick out their necks and speculate from a 'helicopter view' from which some inspiration may be gained for our common tasks; a view to guide socio-economic policies and cooperation between sovereign nations, to guide political parties and to guide research needed to enable all concerned to do the best job possible.

We believe this inspiration can best be gained from the understanding that our diversified tasks must make a contribution to managing our planet. The word 'planet' (that is, the total of all people and all resources available) is used to remind us of the interdependence of our economies and our security we have inherited. No optimal welfare-cum-security is now possible for one continent that is independent of other continents' welfare-cum-security. The word 'manage' is used to remind us of the businesslike character of our tasks. It cannot be denied that the essential goods and services we currently obtain in order to survive are the result of productive enterprises, whose efforts are the outcome of good management. It has become customary in discussions of the best policy for a given country, to suggest that that country has to be run as if it were a corporation: 'Japan, Inc.' or 'Britain, Ltd', etc. In the same spirit our discussion in Part II of this book will be inspired by the concept of 'Planet Earth, Inc.'.

The chapters of Part II have been arranged to start from beginnings that exist and reflect attempts to contribute to world management. Like our integrative approach in Part I, we distinguish a socio-economic and a security component. In the existing institutions contributing to our aims and in the same spirit, and in the international commissions which reported on world-wide issues, the socio-economic component is felt to be the *long-term policies to solve the North–South problem* and these policies will be discussed in Chapter 8. In the same or similar institutions and commissions the security component is identified with the *long-term policies to solve the East–West problem* and these policies will be discussed in Chapter 9.

In both cases the experience of recent decades has taught us that the solutions will not come about automatically. The optimism of *laisser-faire* or of Marxism that an 'invisible hand' or the 'automatism of class struggle' will do the job is not the conclusion of either the Brandt Commission or the Palme Commission (cf. Brandt *et al.*, 1980, 1983; Palme *et al.*, 1982). The attitudes of many governments, political parties and citizens need to be reoriented. Fundamental learning processes will have to be organised. Doctrinaire views will have to be abandoned. We must be prepared to learn from experience. An increasing number of top managers have not only gone through a process of training on the job but have been prepared for their career by a business school (cf. Sturdivant and Adler, 1976).

In Chapter 10 the *learning processes*—different for different governments and for different political parties—will be discussed and their sources discovered.

Beginnings also exist in the field of international cooperation. In fact, a network of attempts exists, often created after a disaster has made us sadder and wiser. The organisation of peace was initially seen as the tasks of a conference, which would be dissolved after they felt they had completed their task. The idea of the need for something lasting found its expression in the building of the Peace Palace (1913) in the Hague, and the Palais des Nations (1937) in Geneva, the latter the seat of the League of Nations. After World War II the United Nations took over a considerable number of existing institutions, whose number grew, for instance after the damage done to the environment had been discovered. In 1985 the United Nations celebrated its fortieth anniversary and the occasion was used by many to rethink the tasks and the instruments needed. The need for strengthening the United Nations will be discussed in Chapter 11.

Whereas the philosophy on which the United Nations institutions is built starts at the top, other processes are at work also, from the base—so-called *integration*. This started centuries ago, and contributed essentially to the ending of armed conflicts. Today (1986) Europe is the focus of this process. Integration as a strategy will be the subject of Chapter 12.

In our concluding chapter, a set of recommendations will be formulated, based on our analysis and directed at our main aim: peaceful coexistence.

7.2   MANAGEMENT INSTITUTIONS

Managing the planet in the optimal way entails the performance of a large number of tasks, by a number of institutions. These institutions may be created by reforming some of the existing United Nations agencies or by creating additional institutions. The choice between reform of existing institutions and the creation of new institutions is best decided by whatever procedure seems most effective. Some guidance may be derived from studying the institutional infrastructure of well-organised countries and from comparative studies of a number of successful corporations.

The establishment of the United Nations agencies was partly inspired by the institutional setup of successfully run nations. This is illustrated by the similarities between UN agencies and national institutions. These similarities are partial only, in some cases for good reasons, in some cases for understandable reasons, even if not justifiably. The UN General Assembly has some features in common with a Parliament; the Security Council with a police force, and many specialised agencies with a country's ministries: the FAO shows similarities with a Ministry of Agriculture; the ILO with a Ministry of Social Affairs; UNESCO with a Ministry of Education; UNCTAD and GATT with a Ministry of International Trade; UNIDO with a Ministry of Industry, and so on.

The parallels often are partial only and in some respects should perhaps not be perfect. One general dissimilarity consists of the lack of power the United Nations agencies have. For a management deserving that name the world institutions must have the power to implement their decisions. Later we shall discuss their tasks, and in some cases these are more limited than the tasks of national ministries.

A good example of what we can learn from a comparison with the institutions of a well-run nation is the management of monetary and financial affairs. In most well-run countries we find a Ministry of Finance (or Treasury), a central bank and an investment bank. Among the UN agencies the International Monetary Fund (IMF) has some tasks in common with a central bank and the World Bank Group (WBG) with an investment bank. The relative importance of the UN agencies is totally different from that of the national institutions, however. In the UN a Treasury hardly exists—each specialised agency has its own small Treasury. The WBG is very important, whereas in many well-run nations there is no public investment bank. IMF as well as central banks are important in both systems, but the IMF lacks some of the powers central banks have.

In our opinion two things can be learned from this comparison. First, the IMF should become a World Central Bank (WCB); and secondly, a World Treasury (WT) should be created. The WT should collect from member countries of the United Nations not only their contribution to the UN Secretariat, but to all UN agencies of which they are members. More important perhaps, part of the financing of Third World development (and development of any world-wide character) should be financed by the WT. In well-run countries a considerable part of development investment is financed by the Treasury's current revenue, avoiding all the complications of loans and debts, and their renegotiation we are now experiencing.

Revenue of the WT should come from world taxes, with all the advantages such a system has for the smooth operation of the optimal order.

Monetary and financial affairs are not the only ones where major changes are desirable. We think another major reform is needed in the system of representation and decision-making. In our opinion the management system of the planet should be integrated into one hierarchy, and here we must learn—as nations must—from well-run corporations. In the long run—that is our perspective—a powerful chief executive board is needed. Also, all activities should be coordinated by one hierarchy consisting of a number of levels and characterised by a workable 'span of control' at the various levels.

Here we want to consider the question of whether the system of 'one nation, one vote' at the UN General Assembly is optimal. The negative attitude of the superpowers *vis-à-vis* the United Nations partly comes from the fact that they feel strongly underrepresented in the Assembly. The number of votes should depend on the size of a nation's population, as in the most advanced democratic Parliaments. Perhaps we should be aware of the previous phases of the most advanced democracies, in which the financial contribution made by a nation should also be reflected in the number of votes. Finally, when considering the viability of nations, we must be aware of the doubtful viability of nations with less than 100,000 inhabitants, or even of those with less than one million inhabitants.

This attempt to reconsider the UN system of representation led us to think of an alternative where, like the Senate of well-run countries, the Executive is responsible to a meeting of a limited number of representatives—say twelve to fifteen—of large units. These units would represent a few of the very large nations—China, India, the USA, the Soviet Union—and regional federations, such as the Organisation of African Unity, an Arab federation, and the European Community. A first subject of research would be the optimal composition of these 'large units', perhaps to be called Regions. Each Region would have as members with varying numbers of votes today's nations. Within the nations the existing levels of decision-making would be taken over. Within the Regions the number of votes would be tied to population size and financial contribution in such a way as to encourage the formation of viable federations of very small units.

A very important new institution to be created is, of course, a UN Police Force. Usually the term UN *Peace* Force is used, but we think 'Police Force' a more appropriate expression for the optimal order, where war as an instrument is no longer applicable.

7.3   LEVELS OF DECISION-MAKING

The management structure we sketched in section 7.2 is an empty box, as long as the functions and powers have not been specified. In a way the structure constitutes what has sometimes been called 'world government'. The fear of and scepticism about that concept are partly caused by incorrect or unformulated ideas about the subjects each institution and each hierarchical level has to deal with. In the present section a number of examples will be discussed in order to present a clearer picture. The criteria to be applied are those set out in section 5.4. As observed before, the optimal levels of decision-making at national or lower levels have, generally speaking, been found and applied. Higher than national levels are avoided by a majority of policy-makers because of a propensity to sovereignty far beyond the optimum. A widespread misunderstanding is that sovereign decision-making means keeping a country's welfare 'in its own hands'. Sovereign decision-making may even negatively affect a country's welfare, since that country is not then represented in the sovereign decision-making of other countries.

The optimal level of decision-making will be higher than national for all problems which affect the welfare of people outside the country, since their welfare is usually given less weight than the decision-making authorities' own people.

For a long time there have been a number of problems whose solution affects more than one nation and where solutions must be based, consequently, on supra-national decision-making. These problems and the way they are best resolved have been listed in the report to the Club of Rome *Reshaping the International Order* (RIO) (Tinbergen *et al.*, 1976). In that report, these problems are listed under the headings: international monetary order, international income redistribution and financing of development, production and (international) distribution of food, international trade and division of labour, (international distribution of) energy, ores and (other) minerals, research and technological development, transnational enterprises, human environment, reduction of armament and ocean management. As a matter of course all types of international economic intercourse belong in this list. More recent subjects are those of the environment and of ocean management. Pollution of the environment has become so acute as a consequence of population growth, the chemical industry and motor traffic that policies to reduce pollution have become necessary. If a country neglects such a policy it not only harms its own citizens, but also those of other countries and so supra-national decision-making is necessary. Oceans contain more resources than fish alone; oil and metal ores from manganese nodules and transportation in oil tankers have become a source of water and beach pollution. Thus the oceans have become a subject for conscientious management.

The corresponding new institution for the environment is the UN Environment Programme (UNEP), but it lacks the power to implement a real international environmental policy. Ocean management has become carefully elaborated in the new Law of the Sea (LoS), formulated in nine years of negotiation, but not yet ratified by the necessary number of member states, as observed before.

7.4 MOST DECISION LEVELS REMAIN THE SAME

The concept of world government meets with widespread aversion and scepticism, as we stated in section 7.3. Aversion and scepticism are largely due to misunderstanding of what an optimal world government means. Some critics seem to think that a world government would replace all existing governments. World government as we conceive it is a supplement to national governments for the solution of a limited number of problems or tasks, as summarised in section 7.3. All other problems or tasks remain at the national or lower levels. Upon inspection it will be found that by far the larger part of decision-making can be left in the hands of those who handle them at present, that is at the national, provincial or municipal level, but also at enterprise or family level. Since decisions often mean decisions on the spending of income, the figures on expenditures at various levels may illustrate our point. If the average tax burden of a representative country is 33 per cent (as it was in the USA in 1982 or in the Netherlands in 1960), this means that the national and lower public authorities together spend one-third, and all lower levels (family, associations, social security agencies) two-thirds of total GNP (cf. Haveman, 1985). Only part of the 33 per cent is spent by the national government and again only part of the latter amount should be spent at supra-national level in an optimal world order. Therefore, these latter expenditures are a modest part only of total expenditures. Similarly, we can anticipate that a modest part of total decision-making only needs to be transferred to higher levels; but, as our listing of the subjects in section 7.3 illustrates, they are decisions on important subjects. This applies, in particular, to security expenditures, where enormous savings can be made as soon as the two superpowers are prepared to cooperate. This presupposes a considerable change in attitute, as observed in section 7.1, and to be discussed more fully in Chapter 10 about learning processes.

7.5 FUNCTIONS AND POWERS OF THE INSTITUTIONS

In the preceding sections we sketched the management structure we think is most appropriate if we seriously want to attain, for the world as a whole, an optimal socio-economic and security order. We took as our prototype, on the one hand, well-run enterprises and countries, and, on the other hand, the rudimentary beginnings made by the United Nations family of institutions.

In the present section we shall discuss some important and generic differences between these two sources which will be our starting point of discussion in Chapter 11: how to strengthen the United Nations institutions. Briefly stated, these differences are to be found in what in United Nations Charters' language are called the 'functions and powers' of the institutions. As a rule these are too limited, although there are differences between individual specialised agencies. Thus, the IMF and the World Bank Group (whose location is not by coincidence Washington, D.C.!) in some respects are fairly powerful. The IMF is able to impose on borrowing countries harsh conditions, which sometimes are even counterproductive.[1] The projects financed by the World Bank itself must be bankable. Both institutions have created additional facilities by which some of the conditions are mitigated and so more adapted to what developing countries are able to agree with, without undermining their development. The institutions lack power in other respects, especially when it comes to mobilising resources, that is imposing on donor countries the contributions to their capital needed in the interest of the world at large. The Brandt Commission's reports are clear enough in this respect; so are previous expert reports, e.g. the Pearson Report (Pearson *et al.*, 1969) and the Tinbergen Report (Tinbergen *et al.*, 1970) and subsequent reports of the United Nations Development Planning Commission (Ramphal *et al.*, 1985). The common feature of all these reports is that they recommend larger contributions from the donor countries. Some of today's serious problems, especially the debt problem[2] of some Latin American countries, would have been considerably more manageable if the Pearson Commission recommendations had been implemented by the industrialised countries. This implementation has been worse the larger the donor countries. The USA and Japan spent about half the percentage of GNP recommended by the various commissions, the middle-sized countries such as West Germany, Britain and France a somewhat higher percentage, and three Scandinavian countries and the Netherlands are the only ones which spent 0.7 per cent of GNP or more (cf. OECD, 1984).

The most dangerous lack of power in comparison to an effective structure is, of course, the Security Council's power, which can be reduced to nothing if one of the permanent members uses its power of veto. In the field of security, practically speaking, the two superpowers are able to impose their will on the rest of the world (cf. Myrdal, 1976). For the lack of something better, a preliminary solution of the world security problem could be organised by them if they were aware of their responsibility to the world at large. The instruments they could use might be adherence to some existing treaties and the signing of new treaties, in particular a ban on the use of weapons in outer space. This option will be discussed in Chapter 9 in more detail.

7.6   PRIVATE BUSINESS AT SUPRA-NATIONAL LEVELS

Our planet's management is not in the hands of public authorities only, although the integrating framework should be a public institution, just as it is in each well-run country. In matters of supra-national management, business leaders have been more advanced than public authorities, as could be anticipated. The creation of multinational—or better, transnational—enterprises preceded the creation of supra-national authorities. They operated in the field of their industrial branches mainly, and were interested in general social structures only if immediately involved—with some personal exceptions for people with a broader vision.

In a way their activities made it possible to liberate themselves from what they considered to be governmental interference in their affairs. In this sense they are trying to profit from the socially less advanced structure in less developed countries or from the socially less advanced structure of international relations between all countries. National public authorities can generally set rules for national enterprises, but foreign governments cannot. This gap in the legal structure of a world subdivided into sovereign states has been cleverly exploited by many transnational enterprises. Because of their greater efficiency they are able to pay higher wages than local enterprises and similarly are able to attract local capital. Often they apply technologies they use in their home region which may not be optimal for the country in which they operate—not optimal, because not all labour can be employed as the consequence of highly capital-intensive technology. Governments of their host countries sometimes even welcome such technologies, for prestige reasons, although their goal is to attain full employment. As long as transnational enterprises are ahead of governments, in matters of international integration an undesirable situation exists in which the supervisory role of government over the area of operations as a whole is incomplete and not concordant with the optimal degree of supervision.

The problem should not, however, be seen as a clash of interests and so as a focus of class struggle. Rather the common

interest of the private and the public sectors and the corresponding common interest of an optimal division of tasks and
responsibilities should be understood and given legal form. This
has been attempted by both the International Chamber of
Commerce and by the United Nations, in the form of 'codes of
conduct' for both transnational enterprises and governments.
For those who hold fast to the priority of national sovereignty
there is no need for codes of conduct for governments; but since
an optimal world order will not necessarily accept absolute
sovereignty, we think such an absolute priority is not part of an
optimal order.

In concluding this section, we emphasise that creativity and
the efficiency of private business should be seen as potential
sources of world welfare and hence as components of the optimal
management of our planet, provided the enterprises concerned
fit into a global framework of legislation covering social, financial
and other matters in the general interest, e.g. environmental
legislation. Transnational enterprises are part of an optimal
world order, but so are codes of conduct.

Wassily Leontief once compared the profit motive of private
enterprise to the sail moving a boat and rules of conduct to the
rudder guiding it. Without the sail the boat would not move.
Without the rudder it might founder on rocks. To guide it safely
to its harbour a boat needs both a sail and a rudder.

7.7 NON-GOVERNMENTAL ORGANISATIONS

In addition to public authorities and enterprises a wide variety
of non-governmental organisations exist which contribute to
human welfare. In section 4.4 we mentioned some which play a
role within nations. There is good reason to discuss them in the
context of international structures, since the international order
is less developed than national social orders. Creative thinking
is more typical of individuals than of organisations and similarly
non-governmental organisations often develop new ideas, propa-
gate them and so contribute to the introduction of original
improvement in official structures. Many forms of international
cooperation found their origin in non-governmental organisations, such as the International Commission of Red Cross
Associations or the European Movement. Contacts between the
Soviet and Western bloc have been made possible first of all by
associations of citizens of both blocs.

Above all else world integration needs to have the groundwork laid by a non-governmental organisation. As before we point to the similarities with like movements at a lower level; in our case the European Movement is probably the best example, but for Latin America the Andes states cooperation may be better known or highlight problems of more concern to Latin American citizens or governments. One of the typical problems for European integration is that of language differences, which hardly exists in Latin America or in the Middle East.

One non-governmental organisation promoting world integration is the Association of World Federalists. But there are some problems they have to solve first. The Association, which was created immediately after World War II, has lost its momentum and is now in the process of being reactivated. This is an internal problem which they hope to solve soon. The changed structure of the military balance between the two superpowers (the US is now no longer superior in power and more vulnerable to strategic missiles but technologically superior in high-tech) requires a modified policy and has made world federalism much more urgent. An effective membership drive to multiply its previous size and influence is promising and is in preparation.

There is also an external problem. Competing organisations exist and this is wasting manpower and money. Integration has to start at home. Some examples of similar organisations are Planetary Citizens (Citoyens du Monde) and the World Constitution and Parliament Association.

NOTES

1. Reduction in public expenditures, often imposed on developing countries by the IMF as a cure for excessive foreign debts, can lead to higher unemployment, economic stagnation and in this way reduce a country's ability to repay its debts, instead of improving it.
2. The debt problem has also been worsened by capital flight, aided by some banks.

REFERENCES

Brandt, W. *et al.* (1980), *North–South: a Programme for Survival*, Pan Books, London and Sydney.

Brandt, W. *et al.* (1983), *Common Crisis, North–South: Co-operation for World Recovery*, Pan Books, London and Sydney.

Haveman, R.H. (1983), *Does the Welfare State Increase Welfare?*, Leiden, Stenfert Kroese.

Myrdal, Alva (1976), *The Game of Disarmament. How the United States and Russia Run the Arms Race*, New York, Pantheon Books.

OECD (1984), *Development Co-operation, Efforts and Policies of the Members of the Development Assistance Committee*, Paris, OECD.

Palme, O. *et al.* (1982), *Common Security. A Blueprint for Survival*, New York, Simon and Schuster.

Pearson, L.B. *et al.* (1969), *Partners in Development*, New York, Washington and London, Praeger.

Ramphal, S.S. *et al.* (1985), *The Challenge to Multilateralism. A Time for Renewal*, United Nations Development Planning Committee, New York.

Sturdivant, F.D. and Adler, L.D. (1976), 'Executives origins: still a gray-flannel world?', *Harvard Business Review* Nov./Dec., pp. 125 ff.

Tinbergen, J. *et al.* (1979), *Towards an Accelerated Development. Propositions for the Second Development Decade*, United Nations Development Planning Committee, New York.

Tinbergen, J. *et al.* (1976), *Reshaping the International Order. A Report to the Club of Rome*, New York, E. P. Dutton.

8   The Socio-Economic Component: Long-Term North–South Policies

8.1   WORLD POVERTY: THE WORLD SOCIAL PROBLEM

In an optimal management of the world two main components can be distinguished which correspond with the two main subjects of this book: economic welfare in the restricted sense, and security. Both components regard all 159 sovereign nations of the world, but their hard core concerns two different groupings of those countries, the *North–South* grouping and the *East–West* grouping. By North–South we mean the prosperous versus the low-income countries, and by East–West we mean the communist-ruled vs. the non-communist ruled.

The main socio-economic problem is how to reduce the difference in welfare. In order to design an appropriate policy *information* is first needed on the existing difference. This cannot be measured by the difference in money (nominal) income per capita. In low-income countries prices are also lower than in high-income countries, because part of what we consume consists of services rendered, (e.g. hairdressing, education, police, etc.). In a World Bank study, Kravis *et al.* (1982) distinguish six income classes among the world's nations, the lowest of which has a real income per capita of 0–14.9 per cent of US income. For those nations the price level of goods is 57 per cent of the US level, the price level of services 21 per cent and the average price level for all domestic products 41 per cent. (For producer durable goods the price level is 130 per cent of the American level.) Consequently the real income per capita is not as low, in comparison to the USA, as the figure expressed in dollars which exchange rates would suggest. For the class of countries cited it is 4.8 per cent for real income per capita and 2.3 per cent for nominal income per capita of US income per capita. Even so it is *less than 5 per cent*. Whereas Western European countries show real per capita incomes between 99 per cent for Norway and 34 per cent for Portugal, most incomes in the developing continents are considerably lower. The figure for India was 6.7 per cent in 1983; in 1970 it was 6.45 per cent, confirming that the ratio changed very little only. South Korea's experience was different, here real income per capita was 11.8 per cent of the US figure in 1970 (cf. Kravis *et al.*, 1982) and 29.4 in 1983. This reflects the rapid development of the Far East, with Japan as its core. In the 1930s Japan could still be considered an underdeveloped country; in 1983 its real income per capita was 80 per cent of the American, with the following figures for the middle-sized European countries:

United Kingdom	76
France	87
West Germany	89
Italy	67

Almost all of Africa and large parts of Asia and Latin America show widespread poverty. The world as a whole now shows the same pattern that we saw in the nineteenth century in the industrialising countries (North America, Europe, Australia); it came to be known as the 'social problem' and gave rise to the socialist movement. At present we are confronted with a world social problem. Neglecting it has been seen to be very dangerous for the world's political stability; it may become more dangerous still.

In order to characterise today's political situation we need to be aware of some important developments in the twentieth century. The socialist movement founded by Marx and his followers split into two main currents: communism and democratic socialism. The countries under a communist régime are the Soviet Union and Eastern European countries, collaborating in the Council for Mutual Economic Assistance (CMEA), China and a few neighbouring countries (North Korea, Vietnam), and Cuba. Communist parties in Western European countries generally have little influence. This influence was more important—up to about one-third of the electorate—in Italy, France and Portugal some 10–20 years ago. In Northern and Central Western Europe democratic socialist parties are the main progressive parties, which have repeatedly been in office. In the USA socialist parties are very weak.

On the world political scene, the communist-ruled nations and the nations with a parliamentary democracy are competing for the adherence of the developing countries. These, however, cooperate in the Group of 77, with over 120 members now, and want to stay outside either the communist or the western 'bloc'.

8.2   DECOLONISATION AND DEVELOPMENT COOPERATION

After World War II the process of decolonisation started, first in Asia where the Japanese helped to start that process. Somewhat later Africa followed. The most humane process of decolonisation was that of India, thanks to Mahatma Gandhi whose philosophy of non-violence showed how far he was ahead of the majority of mankind. Tolerance was his basic attitude, of which we shall have to learn much in future. Fortunately some cultural currents in Britain showed understanding and sympathy for Indian nationalism and the independence of the largest colony of all times was established without a war with Britain. Unfortunately this could not be said about many other liberations. Those of Algeria and Indonesia, for instance, were only obtained after a war. Nevertheless, most colonies were granted independence without a war, after the colonial powers recognised that colonialism had become unacceptable.

By the early 1960s the decolonisation process had brought political independence to large parts of Asia and Africa. Latin America had obtained its political independence much earlier. The three continents together had the common characteristic of poverty, although to different degrees. The liberated countries all became members of the United Nations, increasing the number of sovereign nations threefold, and creating a clear majority of underdeveloped countries. This radically affected the topics dealt with by both the General Assembly and a number of specialised agencies. The World Bank (officially, the International Bank for Reconstruction and Development) gradually shifted its main activity from reconstruction to development. The United Nations Secretariat, under Dr Hans Singer's guidance, prepared the document on the *Development Decade*, adopted in 1961 to mark that decade (1961–70) in which forces should be united to further the economic growth of the low-income countries. The concept of *development cooperation* was coined and an appeal was made to the industrialised member nations to make available, from public means, the additional capital needed for strengthening the infrastructure (road and railway systems, electricity plants and administrative apparatus, among others) deemed necessary for economic growth. Additional means (i.e. what the countries themselves could finance from their savings) often amounted to only some 5 per cent of national income.

The appeal made to the developed countries was not very successful, and the rise in production of some representative underdeveloped economies was disappointing. This led to two initiatives. In 1968 the World Bank set up the Pearson Commission, presided over by Lester B. Pearson, former Prime Minister of Canada. In 1966 the United Nations had already established the UN Development Planning Committee, headed by Jan Tinbergen, Professor of Development Planning at the (then) Netherlands School of Economics. The Pearson Commission reported to donor countries about their contribution to the World Bank, and the UN DPC reported to the UN General Assembly and the Secretariat about the future of world development. In 1970 it recommended a programme for a Second Development Decade (DD II). One of the key figures in both reports was what percentage of GNP should be made available, directly or indirectly, by developed countries' governments to the Third World. The Pearson Commission's recommendation in 1970 was 0.7 per cent, the UNDPC figure 0.75—practically the same figure.

Unfortunately both commissions' recommendations were completely ignored by donor countries, in particular by the larger donor countries. The USA and Japan, the two biggest developed countries, made available no more than *half* of the recommended percentage; the only countries which followed the 0.7 recommendation were Denmark, the Netherlands, Norway and Sweden. The middle-sized countries are somewhere in between (cf. section 7.5).

The necessity of some forms of development cooperation were recognised, in principle, by the 'rich men's club', the Organisation for Economic Cooperation and Development (OECD) in Paris, and thanks to its Development Assistance Committee (DAC) an annual report is available with a wealth of data on the various forms of assistance actually made available.

The lack of response from the large potential donor countries is partly associated with the East–West controversy and the very high armament burden. This constitutes a serious argument in favour of a joint solution of the problems which this book is devoted to.

The highly unsatisfactory development of the Third World economies and the negative attitude of most industrial countries gave rise to yet another initiative. In 1977 a third commission was set up, comprising members with political experience, and presided over by Willy Brandt, former Chancellor of the Federal Republic of Germany and President of the Socialist International. This commission reported in 1980 and again formulated a number of policy measures in order to remedy the hopeless situation in which, after two oil price rises, a large part of the world found itself. Perhaps the most striking feature of this report (cf. Brandt *et al.*, 1980) was that so many of its conclusions were close to the Pearson Commission's. This may be interpreted as showing that no progress whatever towards the goals set (i.e. less inequality between rich and poor countries) had been made between 1970 and 1980. When, after three years, no response worth the name had been made, the Commission published a second report (Brandt *et al.*, 1983), setting out further recommendations. Our conclusion can be illustrated with the figure for real income per capita in India as a percentage of American real income per capita. It hardly changed between 1970 and 1983; from 6.45 to 6.7. A meeting of world political leaders, strongly recommended by the Brandt Commission, was held at Cancún, Mexico, but did not result in any positive policy change. Conservative forces prevailed. A change for the good can only be expected after democratic socialist forces have taken over.

8.3   DEVELOPMENT PLANNING: HOW TO REDUCE THE SCARCITY OF PHYSICAL CAPITAL. TRANSNATIONAL ENTERPRISES

Although macro-planning is not favoured by western industrial countries, and in particular by the USA, they do require planning on the part of their debtors. Similarly the World Bank and the IMF require macro-planning from their debtors. It seems to us that a planned policy is indeed preferable. The shift of emphasis in world economic policy from anti-cyclical policies during the Great Depression to development policies after World War II was reflected in economic science. A true boom in the theory and application of development planning started, and numerous new concepts were launched.

Since planning an economy's development necessarily constitutes a complicated problem cluster, its solution with the aid of one complicated model may be very difficult, if not impossible. A more practical method will, as a rule, be that of successive approximations, often called *planning in stages*. The stages may be called the macro, meso and micro-stage. In the macro-stage estimates are made of the most desirable values, for a series of years, of such macro-variables as total production, total imports and exports, total consumption and total investment (gross and net), total income (gross and net) and total income of a few important social groups. The meso-stage consists of estimates for single industries, chosen in accordance with the economy's structure. The micro-stage consists of single projects, fitting into the meso-plan and submitted for financing to a bank (the World Bank, or a Regional Development Bank) or a foreign government.

Planning in stages may also be applied geographically. Thus, after the macro-plan has been estimated, a geographical meso-stage may refer to the provinces or the states of a federation. Subsequently the micro-stage may deal with single districts or large cities. It is characteristic of planning in stages that the macro-stage may have to be revised on the basis of what is found during the subsequent phases.

As an illustration, consider investment estimates. They may be based, in the first draft, on an average capital:output ratio, i.e. the ratio between investment and the production per annum resulting from that investment. A well-known value for countries as a whole is three years. (The capital:output ratio measures the period whose production is needed to finance the investment.) After the production increase has been decomposed into its branch figures, the investment needed in each branch may be estimated with the capital:output ratios for the single industries. The total of these branch investments will not necessarily yield the original macro capital:output ratio used and enables the planner to revise that figure. Similarly numerous checks can be made and raise the degree of reliability of the plan.

Financing the investments by a foreign bank or government is an example of how the scarcity of physical capital that is characteristic for underdeveloped countries can be reduced. The amounts made available should be geared to the long-term optimal development of the relative incomes per capita of the world's regions and sub-regions, derived with the aid of the concepts and relations described in Chapters 4, 5 and 6. This optimal development cannot be the actual development obtained so far, characterised by a constant ratio of real incomes per capita of India and the USA or similar figures for the world income distribution.

The reduction of the scarcity of physical capital in the Third World may also be brought about by private investment of foreign capital. The most direct form of private investment is that made by *transnational enterprises*, discussed in section 7.6. At the time of writing (1986) the UN Commission on Transnational Corporations had finished a first draft of a *Code of Conduct* to be submitted for approval (cf. Hartzman, 1985).

As discussed before (cf. section 4.1) preferences differ between countries with regard to the ownership of the enterprises needed to develop a nation's productive capacity. In the early years (around 1950) the UN agencies such as the World Bank followed the preferences of many western groups and considered it natural that public investments should concentrate on the creation of infrastructure, anticipating that the superstructure of manufacturing industry would automatically be created by private initiative. The experience of countries such as Turkey and the Netherlands shows, however, that this does not always follow (cf. Tinbergen, 1958).[1] The Dutch State Mines (established in 1902) and the Turkish 'state economic enterprises' (1923) were created because insufficient private capital was available and private enterprise was not prepared to take the perceived risks. For similar reasons state farms were established on newly reclaimed land and after a couple of years sold to private farmers.

An important aspect of a country's economic development is the choice of sectors to be expanded, in particular the nation's industrialisation. As a consequence of increasing productivity in agriculture, manpower becomes available for industrial production. Increased income enhances the demand for industrial products. Depending on the country's raw materials and on the labour-intensity of various manufacturing industries a choice will be made of the most promising industries. Usually the initial phase of the industrialisation process shows a preponderance of textile and clothing industries, because of the labour-intensity, and the availability of cotton, wool or silk. Where raw materials are not available, industrialisation may start by import-substitution, that is home production of finished consumer goods from imported raw materials. For lack of competitiveness this form of industrialisation leads to a weak economy.

One of the goals of industrialisation is a shift of industries from the developed to the less developed economies. The United Nations Industrial Development Organisation (UNIDO) had as its goal that by the year 2000 25 per cent of world manufacturing should be located in the now less developed world (the so-called *Lima target*, formulated in 1975 in the Lima meeting of UNIDO). It is improbable that this goal will be attained, partly because of import impediments of developed countries. Moreover new technological developments make uncertain any estimate of the future structure of world industry and trade.

8.4 INVESTMENT IN HUMAN CAPITAL: CULTURAL ASPECTS OF DEVELOPMENT

It is now known that scarcity of physical capital is not the only cause of underdevelopment. More serious is the scarcity of human capital, that is, of educated and trained manpower. Education was neglected by the authorities in many colonies, particularly in Africa, but also elsewhere. In order to attain higher levels of productivity, in agriculture and mining as well as in manufacturing industry and services (government, education, trade) larger numbers of educated people at all levels are necessary, but they were available in small numbers only. Under colonial regimes the larger part of these occupations were reserved for foreigners. Understandably, following independence a strong preference existed for giving these functions to nationals. However, there was a dilemma in that in order to raise as quickly as possible the number of educated nationals *an increase* in foreign teachers was necessary.

Since the education process is time-consuming, much more so than most physical production processes, nowhere was planning more needed than in education. Consequently particular efforts were made to stimulate this branch of planning and tribute should be paid to what the International Institute for Educational Planning (Paris) has accomplished.

Entrusting education to foreigners may imply the imposition of a foreign culture on students. Even foreign production methods in enterprises may introduce elements of foreign culture, and so creates the problem of whether development cooperation constitutes a threat to the maintenance of the receiving country's culture.

To us the answer seems to consist of four main statements:

(i) As long as development cooperation aims at satisfying the basic needs of the receiving country, the imposition of foreign culture hardly exists, since no culture wants its adherents to starve.

(ii) As soon as some additional welfare beyond that of the basic needs becomes possible the right of cultural freedom should be recognised, provided that
(iii) no aspects of that culture harm other cultural groups.
(iv) Tolerance is a prerequisite of the coexistence of varying cultures.

Although many countries suffer from cultural conflicts and display a high degree of intolerance, development cooperation has not been too impeded by such intolerance. This is due mainly to the basic rule that such cooperation is only established at the receiving country's request. In addition, the execution of development cooperation projects is done voluntarily, either as a gainful employment or based on some combination of idealism and sense for adventure.

The contacts created by it are very useful and, as a rule, widen both parties' horizons. From time to time these contacts may lead to intense discussions, which may help certain features of one's own culture to become critical. People from relatively prosperous countries are by no means always culturally superior— if one can make such comparisons. In many respects the sources of culture are not the sources of well-being.

8.5   INTERNATIONAL TRADE, A NEW INTERNATIONAL ECONOMIC ORDER; INTEGRATION

The most important source of foreign finance is *international trade*; more precisely, the surplus of exports over imports of goods and services. In the first nineteen years after World War II international trade was handled by the General Agreement on Tariffs and Trade, concluded after the failure to create the International Trade Organisation (ITO). In this Agreement initially little attention was devoted to the interests of the Third World. Later this changed, when the Agreement was extended. In the meantime, in 1964, a new specialised UN agency was established as a result of Raúl Prebisch's research and campaign in favour of the Third World. The new agency was called the *United Nations Conference on Trade and Development* (UNCTAD), and was established to discuss the basic problems of development in relation to trade and the policies to be recommended in order to create trading conditions more favourable to development. Thus, UNCTAD's discussions and negotiations contributed to the stabilisation and strengthening of commodity markets, to the creation of preferences for imports from developing countries into developed countries, to a programme for the least developed countries, to the more satisfactory transfer of technology, to furthering shipping by developing countries, to the extension of trade between countries with different social systems and of trade between developing countries (cf. United Nations, 1985).

The unsatisfactory response of the developed countries to the appeals made to them during the 1960s and the early 1970s, and the additional difficulties caused to the non-oil-exporting developing countries led to an initiative taken by a group of countries presided over by Algeria to convene a special session of the UN General Assembly on 'Raw Materials and Development', which met in April 1974. This Sixth Special Session produced a Declaration and a Programme of Action (cf. Kaufmann, 1980, p. 81) on the definition of and the action to attain a *New International Economic Order*, in which the position of the developing countries would be ameliorated, in fact become less unequal than they felt they were under the prevailing order. Among other things, larger capital transfers, higher prices for their products (in particular for raw materials) and more voting rights in the World Bank and IMF were characteristic of this innovation. In the autumn of 1975 the Seventh Special Session of the General Assembly was held on Development and International Economic Cooperation. This resulted in a real consensus with a new programme of work, which was welcomed by the US permanent representative, Mr D. Moynihan.

Unfortunately the subsequent development did not reflect the continuation of this promising start. In most developed countries progressive governments were followed by conservative ones (US, UK, West Germany) and the *détente* between the superpowers was overtaken by a new confrontation. No elaboration of the NIEO was undertaken and, as already stated, attempts by the Brandt Commission, established on 28 September 1977, to continue world-wide negotiations did not succeed. Even in the symposium held on 28–29 November 1984 (cf. United Nations, 1985a) to mark UNCTAD's twentieth anniversary this was all that could be concluded by J.P. Pronk, then Deputy Secretary General of UNCTAD.

We agree with the speakers at that symposium, most of whom considered the Brandt Commission's recommendations as the guide to an optimal international development policy.

An additional remark on the role of international development cooperation is that cooperation between developing countries should assume a special form for small developing countries. Since the smallest countries in this category are hardly viable as sovereign states, integration constitutes the best development policy. This is true in particular for small developing countries clustered in one region, the most important example being the Caribbean–Central American region. Although various attempts to integrate the Caribbean islands have failed, we are convinced that integration remains the formula to apply. Renewed attempts are recommended and the strategy we suggest is that a start be made by the smallest units. By uniting they should try to become economically stronger and so to become 'worth while' for the somewhat larger units to start negotiations with. The United Nations—and UNCTAD in particular—might assist by carrying out the economic analyses needed, in particular analyses of the industrial specialisation to strive for. We recommend that the Central American nations should also join in the process. In view of the present political tendencies it is obvious that the process can only be achieved in the longer term. It may help to reduce the degree of nationalism now prevailing.

In other parts of the world too, especially in Africa, integration of neighbouring countries may be a creative alternative to concentrate on, in order to reduce the unproductive political controversies existing between so many neighbouring countries. At the same time greater internal autonomy to deal with purely local problems can reduce tension between different cultural groups.

8.6   BALANCE OF PAYMENTS ASSISTANCE, IMF CONDITIONS AND THE DEBT PROBLEM

The protracted stagflation in the West, the tendencies to protectionism and the redistribution caused by the oil price increases have contributed to the trade deficits experienced by most Third World countries. Large credits have been offered by private banks which have accumulated to enormous debts in several developing countries. Others applied for credits from the IMF.

The IMF usually applies a model valid for single countries in balance of payments difficulties, which we call the imposition of a deflationary policy.[2] This model can be supplemented by additional facilities created for countries that are the victim of external forces (energy prices, exceptionally low prices of their export products) and these supplements constitute a softening of otherwise severe conditions.

A different situation develops if a large number of debtor countries are all asked to follow a deflationary policy. Then additional problems to the others are created by the Fund's conditions (cf. Holland's and Chakravarty's papers in the 1984 UNCTAD symposium, United Nations, 1985a). Again the Brandt Commission's 1983 recommendation (Brandt *et al.*, 1983) applies, to double the SDR volume in circulation, instead of the 47 per cent increase actually performed.

8.7   TECHNICAL ASSISTANCE; APPROPRIATE TECHNOLOGY

Alongside the scarcity of physical and human capital, underdeveloped countries suffer from a scarcity of technological knowledge. In order to fill this lacuna, information on technology may contribute to a country's optimal development. Two main flows of such information are supplied: one by private investors, especially transnational enterprises, and one by technical assistance, supplied by the United Nations Development Programme (UNDP) or bilaterally by governments of developed countries through technological advisers.

A major problem involved is what technological information is optimal. Initially transnational enterprises and individual advisers almost automatically supplied information about the technology they were using in their own country. This was also the preference of the governments and citizens of the receiving countries, because they were impressed by modern technologies, thinking that their application would automatically create the level of well-being prevailing in the donor countries.

This is a misunderstanding since the results of a technology depend on the availability of physical and human capital. If a developing country produces with the aid of capital-intensive technology it may not be able to compete on the world market, because capital is scarcer than in developed countries and hence more expensive. In many cases the workers may not be sufficiently skilled to use the capital-intensive method. In addition fewer workers will be employed, since the quantity of capital available is not sufficient to employ all workers. Gradually it has been understood that, as a rule, in developing countries other technologies will be optimal and so more appropriate than in developed countries.

The Dutch transnational enterprise Philips Lamps NV runs a pilot enterprise in Utrecht where alternative technologies are being tried out.

Appropriate technology is dependent on several factors not usually discussed in economic textbooks, these are largely of a technical nature, such as quality of the product, the quantity held in stock and the optimal size of one run of the product to be produced before the machines used are set (lot size) (cf. Boon, 1978, 1981).

Important new problems and new solutions are being introduced by the recent technological revolution created by the use of micro-electronic devices. 'Computerisation' and 'automation' open up wide new horizons which threaten large groups of workers in developed as well as less developed countries. The threat is directed in particular at unskilled workers and hence at developing countries, but also at entire branches of activity that can be replaced by the new technologies.

In principle, automation could be used to increase the total amount of goods produced worldwide, and increase everyone's living standard. But under current economic systems the potential benefits often accrue only to a few entrepreneurs and to consumers at the expense of displaced workers, who will then naturally oppose these new technologies. Through the creation of new employment opportunities these benefits could and should be spread more equally.

When container shipping, which can eliminate a great deal of burdensome work, was introduced in the United States, the dockworkers staged a crippling four-month strike, out of fear of becoming unemployed. Japanese enterprises usually do not dismiss their workers when they introduce a labour-saving technology, but retrain them and re-employ them in better paying jobs. In this way, workers are motivated to search for ways to make their own present jobs unnecessary, because they share in the resulting benefits. Such policies are also in the interest of entrepreneurs, because it enables them to introduce new technologies more rapidly.

In a large empirical study on the penetration of the new technologies in a number of Latin American countries, Boon arrives at the conclusion that this penetration is higher than anticipated by many economists since the quality of products requires computerised equipment such as numerically controlled machine tools (Boon, 1986).

8.8 SELF-RELIANCE AS A CORE OF DEVELOPMENT

Somewhat as a reaction to the concept of development through cooperation, it has been understood by those involved that alongside the subjects so far discussed, the role of the developing peoples themselves is at the heart of the process. Before the forms of cooperation discussed took the institutional shapes described, production, consumption and distribution took place and the larger part—more than three-quarters—of, for instance, investments were made by nationals of the countries of the Third World. The most desirable development for all concerned, as a matter of course, is development by the people concerned, in their own way, and as an expression of creativity and confidence in their own capabilities. All that can be done to stimulate self-confidence and creativity should be part of a development policy. Also here the role of schooling must be emphasised, and hence the creation of human capital. In this respect a country's or a people's culture fosters attitudes that may be more favourable to economic development in one case than in another. A well-known case in the United States are the so-called Pennsylvania Dutch, a community which holds to all sorts of antiquated means of production and habits. Obviously there are cultures which attach less importance to material welfare than others. Moreover, there are individuals within the same culture, people or race who are more materialistic than others. Thus, the larger part of America's white population is of European origin, but on the average they are more enterprising than the individuals of the same European countries who stayed in Europe. Of course the circumstances in which they grew up influenced their decision to emigrate: part of the Irish left during the potato famine of the 1840s, to quote one well-known example.

Similar considerations may be applied to other parts of the world. One could even venture an heroic generalisation and formulate the hypothesis that the underdeveloped parts of the world are those of oldest settlement: from there the most enterprising individuals spread across the empty, or almost empty, regions, where the quantity of natural resources per person generally surpasses the quantity in the areas of oldest settlement. Easy generalisations are dangerous, though.

8.9   CONCLUDING REMARKS

In this chapter an attempt has been made to outline a group of political measures aimed at reaching a path of optimal development towards an optimal socio-economic order, as set out in Chapters 4, 5 and 6. We found that in the 1980s little progress towards an optimal world socio-economic order has been made. Such an optimal order would give a higher standard of living in the low-income continents (Africa, Asia and Latin America) in comparison to the high-income continents. Partly this will become possible if expenditures on armaments are reduced—an aspect to be discussed in Chapter 9. But also the socio-economic policy instruments themselves can make larger contributions. Population growth can and must be reduced, the pollution of the natural environment must be kept under stricter control. With the aid of technological creativity more welfare will be derived from a given quantity of resources. The socio-economic management of our planet can be improved considerably by the creation of some twelve to fifteen federations, cooperating in one world federation. A limited but important set of decisions will have to be made at the world level and authorities will have to be given the competence and the power to implement their decisions. The large majority of decisions on socio-economic policy remain in the hands in which they are now, but lessons from the past must contribute to make wiser decisions. For these decisions the sovereignty of individual nations can and should be maintained. But for decisions affecting other nations or continents it is in our own interest that sovereignty be shifted to higher levels. Only then is it possible for our own nation to avoid becoming the victim of what other nations could decide— by deciding jointly.

NOTES

1. As an illustration of what at that time was the opinion of the World Bank's President it may be recorded that this report was published three years after its completion.
2. Even in this case it is not always clear whether the Fund's counsellors are aware of the irrelevance to reduce a country's expenditures on non-tradables, such as primary education, health care and construction, with the purpose of improving its balance of payments.

REFERENCES

Boon, G.K. (1978), *Technology and Sector Choice in Economic Development*, Alphen aan den Rijn, Sijthoff and Noordhoff.
—— (1981), *Technology Transfer in Fibres, Textile and Apparel*, Alphen aan den Rijn and Rockville, MD, Sijthoff and Noordhoff.
—— (1986), *Computer-Based Techniques: Diffusion, Impact and Policy in the South–North Perspective* (forthcoming).
Brandt, W. *et al.* (1980), *North–South*, London and Sydney, Pan Books.
—— (1983), *Common Crisis*, London and Sydney, Pan Books.
Hartzman, R. (1985), 'Close to an agreement', *Development Forum*, New York, United Nations.
Kaufmann, J. (1980), *United Nations Decision Making*, Alphen aan den Rijn and Rockville, MD, USA, Sijthoff and Noordhoff.
Kravis, I.B. (1986), 'The Three Faces of the International Comparison Project', *The World Bank Research Observer* 1, pp. 3–26.
Kravis, I.B. *et al.* (1982), *World Product and Income*, World Bank, Baltimore, Johns Hopkins Press.
Tinbergen, J. (1958), *The Design of Development*, The Economic Development Institute, International Bank for Reconstruction and Development, Baltimore, Johns Hopkins Press.
United Nations (1985), *The History of UNCTAD*, New York, United Nations.
—— (1985a), *The Development Dialogue in the 1980s — Continuing Paralysis or New Consensus?* New York, United Nations.

9 The Security Component: Long-Term East–West Policy

9.1 HISTORICAL BACKGROUND

In this chapter the security component of the world's policy for optimal development will be discussed. The hard core of such a world policy is a policy for peaceful coexistence of the eastern and the western blocs. If this policy can be formulated and pursued the other—numerous—security aspects will become tractable, at least in the long run. Some of the regional conflicts that threaten the world's security do so because the parties involved are now able to solicit the assistance of one of the two superpowers. In an attempt to set the stage of the present security problems we shall describe the evolution of what originally seemed to be a part of human nature, an aspect of mankind's society, but gradually deviated more and more from anything deserving the qualification 'humane'. Whereas human intellect, applied to the fields of technology and management as well as to the fields of satisfying refined and subtle needs, has made possible a happier world population and a planetary society without war, vice, errors and mismanagement have led us in the opposite direction. There is a real threat of the complete annihilation of civilisation and the larger part of the natural environment. The process of evolution, from elementary atoms through increasingly complex organic molecules, to living beings of ever more capabilities, up to the awesome creativity of the finest artists and scientists might, then, finish in self-destruction.

How in this, the most crucial, chapter of our study, did we arrive on this track, and is it possible to head for the optimal destination by shifting course?

In primitive human society fighting was one activity to satisfy basic needs, both physical and psychical, and physical strength was the most important instrument: a fully labour-intensive activity. It remained so when complemented by mental capabilities. Soon enough means of production such as axes introduced a modest element of capital, as did the use of horses. A next step brought protection with shields and armour. Warships are another form of military capital. Single men united into groups and later formed armies. Armies could be hired and the Swiss, before becoming peaceful watchmakers, engineers and hoteliers, often fought as mercenaries for foreign rulers. Capital goods changed their character after explosives were invented, to manufacture guns, and economies of scale enlarged them. Manpower was enlarged by the introduction of conscription, forcing young men to fight even against their will. The father of economics, Adam Smith, discussed this militarisation and even called it the 'finest of arts', probably thinking of the courageous soldiers who risked their life or health to defend their nation. Whether the same qualification applies to an offensive war remains controversial, to say the least.

Alongside the non-volunteers *non-combatants* were drawn into the process. Some outsiders—nurses,[1] doctors, the organisers of the Red Cross[2] (or Red Crescent, in Islamic societies)—started to devote themselves to non-war activities. Some legal protection of the victims was introduced, still leaving intact the 'duty' of the conscript to participate in the war industry.

Individual authors introduced other ideas: 'die Waffen nieder' (down with weapons) wrote Bertha von Suttner (1843–1914; Nobel Peace Prize, 1905). These individuals showed their abhorrence and acted accordingly. Then politicians began to act, in the Peace Conferences of 1899 and 1907 in The Hague, leading to the building of the Peace Palace in that same city, now the seat of the International Court of Justice.

That palace had been hardly inaugurated when World War I broke out, as an almost unavoidable chain of events set in motion by the assassination at Serajevo of Austria-Hungary's crown prince. So many nations were involved, as a consequence of the increased international links and rivalries, that the name *World War* was justified—the more so because several countries' colonies were drawn into the struggle. The most dreadful feature of this 'Great War' perhaps was the trench warfare in Belgium, which had been drawn into the war by the German violation of its neutrality. Innumerable young Europeans were killed and very many others crippled. The revolutions in Russia and Germany closed this tragedy, bringing to power the Communists in Russia and Social Democrats in Germany.

Peace conditions were imposed on Germany by the Western Allies which, as predicted by the famous economist John Maynard Keynes (1920), would disorganise the German economy and might lead to another conflict. Keynes, then 36 years old, was unable to persuade the older negotiators, but unfortunately was perfectly right. As a consequence of the Versailles Peace Treaty imposed on the Weimar Republic, its economy was forced into a hyperinflation, leading to an impoverishment of the middle classes. From 1924–29 there was a recovery, but in 1929 a world depression (later called the Great Depression) started and precipitated an unprecedented level of unemployment. Hitler gained widespread allegiance. By an unhappy combination of coincidences he understood how to manoeuvre himself into a dictatorial position of power. One of the unhappy coincidences was that he had good economic advisers and succeeded in quickly reducing unemployment which brought him much support and enabled him to remilitarise Germany ahead of other European countries and start World War II according to (his) plan. It did not end, however, according to his plan. The Allied forces were victorious—in particular, the Soviet Union. With the aid of tactical moves—non-aggression treaties, first with Hitler (1939) and later with the western democracies (1941), and with an unprecedented sacrifice of human life, the Soviet Union was able to counter the Nazis and to come out of the war stronger: the Soviet Union's sphere of influence shifted westward, to include East Germany, Poland, Hungary, Romania and Bulgaria, followed in 1948 by Czechoslovakia.

World War II was even crueller than World War I. Warfare had developed into 'total war' and, among other features, all citizens were considered enemies and treated accordingly. Residential quarters became bombing targets, alongside military objects. Moreover, on the Nazi side an abhorrent racist target was pursued which placed 'national socialism' outside human civilisation.

But World War II was fought by the Western Allies too as a total war: Dresden was needlessly bombed and the first atomic bombs were dropped on Hiroshima and Nagasaki. In fact, the discovery of processes to harness nuclear energy, and the present quantities available, has brought a qualitative mutation of the military instrument that requires a rethinking of the possibilites and the choices of warfare.

As a result of this very briefly sketched history of the evolution of war the starting point of any future security policy may be summarised as follows. The main opponents in today's (1986) world are the United States and the Soviet Union (US and SU). Their conflicting aims are partly ideological and may be seen as an opposed view on the degree of centralisation of the economy, and partly geopolitical. Former Chancellor of the Federal Republic of Germany, Helmut Schmidt, thinks the latter element to be stronger than the former. The most threatening arms of the two main opponents ironically are a heritage of Hitler's rockets and are offensive. The arsenals of the SU and the US, although perhaps of comparable strength, are different in composition. The SU in 1983 had twice the number of tanks as the US, and eight times as many chemical weapons; their annual production of ballistic missiles is five times the US annual production (Berkhof, 1985).

The US has eleven aircraft carriers compared to the SU's one. It is considered to be stronger in micro-electronics, and the present administration favours a research programme known as the Strategic Defence Initiative (SDI) aimed at defence against missile attacks, which may well lead to an arms race in outer space.

9.2 SECURITY POLICY ACTIVITIES OF THE UNITED NATIONS (WORLDWIDE OR REGIONAL)

The threat to world security is generally acknowledged and in recent decades numerous initiatives to avoid it have been taken in various quarters. In this chapter these initiatives will be summarised as a starting point to arrive at proposals for a future security policy. This summary will be presented under two headings: what has been done in the framework of the United Nations (UN) and what has been done bilaterally by the SU and the US. This section deals with UN activities. These consist of meetings with the aim of drawing up treaties. In the UN the final-step meetings are those of the General Assembly (GA) and, as far as security is concerned, the Security Council (SC) (cf. Kaufmann, 1980). GA meetings may be the regular annual sessions or special sessions. Of the latter type two—the tenth (1978) and the twelfth (1982)—were devoted to disarmament. Disarmament and other security issues may, however, also be on the agenda of annual meetings. We shall also report on regional meetings and treaties.

The results of past discussions of the many aspects of security may be summarised by a chronological list of treaties concluded:

Table 9.1 Treaties concluded in the UN framework

1959	Antarctic Treaty
1963	Partial Test Ban Treaty
1967	Outer Space Treaty
1970	Non-Proliferation Treaty (NPT) enters into force
1971	Tlatelolco Treaty; Seabed Treaty
1975	Biological War Treaty
1975	Final Act, Helsinki Conference on Security and Cooperation in Europe (CSCE); First Review Conference of the NPT
1977	Belgrade follow-up to Helsinki CSCE
1978	Protocol I added to Geneva Conventions of 1949 on environment modification (ENMOD)
1979	UN Moon Agreement
1980	Second Review Conference of the NPT
1982	Madrid follow-up to Helsinki CSCE
1984	First Review Conference on ENMOD
1985	Third Review Conference of the NPT

Restricting ourselves to the more important of the agreements listed, we do not deal with the Antarctic Treaty (1959) and the Moon Agreement (1979). The 1963 Partial Test Ban Treaty deals with the important issue of stopping the testing of new weapons. Under the 1963 Treaty not all testing is banned, but testing in the atmosphere, in outer space and under water. A comprehensive test ban has not yet been agreed upon.

The 1967 Outer Space Treaty deals with the principles governing the activities of states in the exploration and use of outer space, including the moon and other celestial bodies (Kaufmann, p. 84). It was followed by other agreements, prepared by the same committee, established in 1959 (the GA Committee on the Peaceful Uses of Outer Space). Another agreement in this series is the UN Moon Agreement (1979) mentioned before. The committee also discusses 'remote sensing'; that is, the remote observation of relevant objects and more particularly from the atmosphere and outer space (cf. Voûte, 1985), which is of considerable economic and security importance.

The Non-Proliferation Treaty (NPT) aims at a containment of nuclear arms to the countries which are already in the possession of such arms and the limitation of these arms where they exist. As a *quid pro quo* the countries not having nuclear arms will be assisted in obtaining nuclear energy for peaceful purposes. The 1985 Third Review Conference found the Treaty to be operating 'satisfactorily'. The doubtful significance of the NPT for the struggle against nuclear arms is set out, however, by Alva Myrdal (1976). Even so, in 1985, the non-nuclear, neutral and non-aligned member countries succeeded in exerting considerable pressure on the US, the United Kingdom and France to participate in the urgent negotiation of a Comprehensive Test Ban Treaty (cf. Epstein, 1986).

The Tlatelolco Treaty aims at keeping Latin America nuclear-free. Argentina, Brazil, Chile and Cuba have declared themselves not bound to it, however. It was drafted by the Mexican, Alfonso García Robles, who received the Nobel Peace Prize in 1982.

The 1971 Seabed Treaty aimed at keeping the seabed nuclear-free. Its relative importance will grow after the new Law of the Sea has been ratified by the necessary number of states: then the positive use of the seabed will have been identified and agreed upon.

The 1975 Biological War Treaty attempts to limit the use of bacteriological weapons. Although verification is so difficult that it has not been provided for in this treaty, the American stocks of these arms have been destroyed.

The meetings of Helsinki, Belgrade and Madrid are regional and deal with security and cooperation in Europe. Although formally agreement on a number of principles has been attained this does not contribute to a real solution of the East–West tension in Europe: the meaning of expressions such as 'human rights' are interpreted by both sides in their own way.

Protocol I, added in 1978 to the 1949 Geneva Conventions, deals with military techniques that modify the environment, to which limitations are set. The First Review Conference in 1984 stated that these have so far been effective. There are 45 members. The next review conference will not be held before 1989.

Important debates on security issues and especially on disarmament have been held in Geneva since 1962, first in the Eighteen Nations Disarmament Committee (ENDC), later enlarged to 26 members (1969) and to 31 members; its name having changed several times and finally (1984) called *Conference on Disarmament* (CD). Its report to the GA traditionally became one of the main substantive reports before the GA's First Committee (Kaufmann, p. 33). The CD is chaired alternately by one of the superpowers. Important contributions to CD's deliberations have been made by the Swedish delegate Alva Myrdal and her successor Inga Thorsson. Not much progress towards disarmament has so far been made. This has been highlighted in Myrdal's famous book, *The Game of Disarmament*, sub-titled *How the United States and Russia Run the Arms Race*. Based on an impressive amount of factual documentation, the superpowers are accused of playing a game with the rest of the world and being interested exclusively in their own arms race. Five years after the publication of this book, in July 1981, Inga Thorsson made an eloquent summary of the state of affairs in the last full session before the GA Special Session on Disarmament II to which the CD was to report. To paraphrase, she said: 'Do the leading military powers have the *sincere will* to achieve the goals they supported three years ago? ... And so here we sit, all bilateral arms negotiations suspended and their commitment to multilateral arms negotiations doubtful.' Among the points made and the questions attached the following issues are dealt with.

With regard to European Theatre Nuclear Forces (TNF) serious negotiations are still not in sight. Agreement to reduce them will be infinitely more difficult. The Swedish government has never believed that the dual deployment of SS-20s and Pershing and cruise missiles are necessary to maintain the existing rough equilibrium. We have, therefore, the right to request that TNF negotiations start without further delay.

On SALT II she repeated her demand to both superpowers to respect the provisions of SALT II.

She then made a *tour d'horizon* of the other items, each supposed to be entrusted for consideration to *ad hoc* working groups. On the elaboration of a Comprehensive Disarmament Programme under the chairmanship of Ambassador García Robles she was satisfied. On the establishment of negative security assurances she considered it encouraging that under the chairmanship of Minister Ciarrapico the corresponding working group was seeking a formula to assure non-nuclear weapon states against the use or threat of use of nuclear weapons. Only coordinated and binding undertakings by the nuclear weapon states are satisfactory, however. The unilateral declarations so far made only benefit the nuclear weapon states and their allies. This is unacceptable. In April 1981 Ambassador Lidgard asked the nuclear weapon states' representatives to confirm that the states outside their alliances and committed to a permanent nuclear weapon-free status be exempted from the use or the threat of use of nuclear weapons: 'We have not yet received any answer.'

The issue dealt with in the third working group, on banning

radiological weapons, is an example of the limited importance which the superpowers attribute to the CD. The draft Radiological Weapons Treaty they put before the Committee completely lacks substance. A prohibition on the attack against nuclear installations should be added to the draft. The drafters would do well to listen more carefully to the arguments in favour of such a prohibition.

The subject of chemical weapons, dealt with in the fourth *ad hoc* working group, needs to enlarge a prohibition on production and stockpiling of chemical weapons.

Unfortunately some working groups don't exist, especially one on a comprehensive weapon test ban. Some delegations of nuclear weapon states still refuse to enter multilateral negotiations on the highest priority of our agenda, disregarding their own votes in favour of such a step in the UNGA. Another concerns stopping the nuclear arms race and nuclear disarmament. In both cases Sweden associates itself with the Group of 21.

Finally Mrs Thorsson expresses the need to add to the CD agenda the subject of the military use of outer space. To sum up, official disarmament negotiations, the success of which is so desperately needed, show a dismal record and we know where to place the blame for it.

The general public is beginning to lose patience and increasingly shows this, in a quickly growing peace movement. On their side they find eminent experts like George F. Kennan. Weapons are no longer a means to security; they have become a threat to security.

We have given an unusual amount of space to Mrs Thorsson's address, since we believe it to be a clear exposé of today's *problématique*. Between 1981 and 1986 not much progress was made.

The 40th meeting of the GA (1985) adopted a resolution on the Prevention of an Arms Race in Outer Space in which all states are called upon to contribute actively to the peaceful use of outer space and the superpowers urged to pursue intensively their bilateral negotiations. The CD is requested to deal with the subject and report to the 41st (1986) GA.

Simultaneously with the CD meetings in Geneva, discussions have been going on in Vienna, which started as long ago as 1973, on the Mutual Balanced Force Reductions (MBFR) in Central Europe. Involved are East Germany (DDR), Poland, Czechoslovakia, West Germany (FRG), Belgium, the Netherlands and Luxembourg (Benelux), and the countries with armed forces based in these countries: the SU, US, Britain and Canada. The intention was to reach an agreement on a two-phased reduction to 900,000 on both sides, of which 700,000 would be land forces. After countless meetings no agreement has been reached. Most of the discussions dealt with differences of opinion about the number of men actually present in the area.

Finally, as a follow-up of the Helsinki–Belgrade–Madrid 35-state conferences, in Stockholm negotiations on confidence and security-building measures and disarmament in Europe took place between 1984 and 1986, concluding with some modest agreements in 1986.

Our summary of the multilateral negotiations provides a clear picture of the stalemate the world is in, mainly as the consequence of the distrust between the superpowers, whose points of view at least up to 1986 were hopelessly rigid on the main issues: social system and arms reduction. It is obviously their responsibility to find a way out of this impasse, from which the world at large, but also they themselves may become the victims.

9.3 SECURITY POLICY BILATERAL ACTIVITIES OF THE SU AND THE US

As set out in the preceding section the superpowers are so preoccupied with their bilateral problems that they prefer to ignore multilateral relations, except to some extent those between their alliances, NATO and the Warsaw Pact. One excuse is the one nation, one vote system of the UN and many of the UN institutions, to which we shall address ourselves in Chapter 11, in particular. So let us now look at what bilateral negotiations have led to. So far those have resulted in some agreements now to be discussed. In 1963 the Hot Line Agreement was concluded, establishing the possibility of consultation at the highest level with the aid of a direct telegraphic connection. In 1971 this was technically improved. Such consultation may serve to reduce the impact of misunderstandings or errors in the communication techniques used.

Around 1970 a period of détente contributed to the Strategic Arms Limitation Talks (SALT I). Strategic arms are the missiles able to hit directly the other party's territory, a capability created by the Intercontinental Ballistic Missiles (ICBMs). The talks led to the most important treaty so far concluded, the Anti-Ballistic Missile (ABM) Treaty. Its main aim is to limit the attempts made on both sides to switch to a defensive system against ICBM attacks. It is tragic that the superpowers, both presenting themselves as peace-loving nations, after the War started to copy an aggressor (Hitler), instead of concentrating on defensive weapons from the start. Once offensive strategic missiles are deployed, switching to a defensive system (transarmament) implies the danger of one party attaining a first-strike capacity because it believes it is protected against retaliation. Hence it can only be undertaken jointly and hardly so at all under present circumstances. The ABM Treaty limits defensive weapons to 100 on both sides, at no more than two sites; in 1976 this was reduced to one site. One of the useful institutions created is the Standing Consultative Commission, where interpretations and amendments to the treaty can be and have been discussed—a modest contribution to more mutual confidence. Under the treaty military satellites for reconnaissance, surveillance, early warning and communications are permitted and called 'national technical means of verification'. Developing, testing, or deploying anti-ballistic-missile system or any component that is sea-based, air-based, space-based or mobile land-base is banned. Only fixed land-based systems or components are permitted. 'Modernisation' is also permitted. 'Exotic' sophisticated technologies, such as lasers or particle beams, must not be used—according to the 1984 version—unless the parties consult and amend the Treaty (cf. Chayes, Chayes and Spitzer, 1985).

The second agreement concluded in 1972 is known as the Interim Agreement on the Limitation of Strategic Offensive Arms. The limits set are so high and leave open so many loopholes (e.g. MIRVing), that this agreement is hardly relevant (cf. Myrdal, 1976, p. 105).

In 1972 also the Agreement on Naval Vessels Information was concluded. The acronym ABM was changed to BMD—ballistic missile defence.

In 1974 the Threshold Test Ban Treaty (TTBT) was concluded between US and SU. Tests could go on until 31 March 1976, but from that date were limited to 150,000 tons (ten times the power of the Hiroshima bomb). This too can hardly be taken seriously (cf. Epstein, 1976).

Finally, in 1979, a further limitation was agreed upon (SALT II). This treaty was not ratified by the American Senate, however, and in late 1986 the US exceeded the negotiated limits.

In 1981 the SU presented a draft treaty in the UN banning all anti-satellite (ASAT) activities. When in 1983 the US had still not replied Richard Garwin, Kurt Gottfried and retired admiral Noel Gayler drafted an alternative text and presented it to the US Senate Foreign Relations Committee. In that same year the SU presented a new draft, which incorporated most of the concerns expressed by the three men (cf. Garwin, 1984). In his address to a UN Symposium (26 January 1984) the last author expressed the hope that one feature of the SU 1983 draft could be changed in negotiations. He added that otherwise it would be an enormous progress (in the interest of US and international security) to have a treaty banning all ASAT weapons from space, all ASAT tests and the use of force against space and from space to earth.

It was also in 1983 (23 March) that President Reagan launched his Strategic Defence Initiative (SDI). As is well known, this initiative is aimed at research to find a defence against an ICBM attack. Most independent scientists doubt whether such a technology can actually be invented. The implication is that the party which first invents the technology attains a first-strike capability. Autonomous research of the two superpowers constitutes a new arms race. The only alternative is joint research, which, if successful, could contribute to common security.

On 6 August 1985, the SU began a unilateral moratorium on all nuclear tests and invited the US to join it. The Reagan administration refused, saying that periodic tests of existing nuclear stockpiles were necessary to be certain of their continued reliability. But high reliability is needed only in a first strike, where every weapon must work, because otherwise surviving enemy missiles could retaliate. To deter a nuclear attack through the threat of retaliation high reliability is not needed. Even the fear that only a portion of the nuclear weapons launched in retaliation would work would be a formidable deterrent against an attempted first strike. Above all, a potential aggressor could never be sure that every weapon of the opponent would fail to explode because it had not been tested for a long time. In this way a comprehensive test ban would reduce the instability of nuclear deterrence, by casting doubt on the chances of success of a first strike, without weakening the deterrent effect of the threat of a retaliatory second strike (cf. section 9.7).

On 15 January 1986, General Secretary Gorbachev proposed a treaty to eliminate all nuclear weapons by the year 2000. President Reagan has said that it contained some positive elements, but has not yet responded to the full Soviet proposal. Gorbachev offered to eliminate, in a first phase, all SU medium-range missiles in Europe in return for an elimination of US medium-range missiles stationed in Europe, leaving French and British missiles unchanged. The SU gave up its earlier demands that French and British nuclear forces be balanced by SU medium-range missiles, and accepted the long-standing US position that the US could not negotiate on behalf of the French and British. The US government then came back and said it was now also negotiating on behalf of the Japanese and Chinese, and demanded an additional reduction in Soviet medium-range missiles in Asia. Whether the SU will make further concessions and accept this new demand, remains to be seen (cf. section 13.9).

9.4 PRESENT WAR THREATS: A SUMMARY

Let us now briefly summarise what threats mankind faces at the time of writing (1986).

First of all the world–and in particular the two superpowers— have an enormous over-capacity of weapons capable of killing all mankind and much other life several times over. According to some estimates nuclear weapons with an explosive power of 100 megatons would suffice to produce a 'nuclear winter': some 16,000 megatons are stockpiled (Sagan, 1983).

Secondly, the arms race continues, both quantitatively and qualitatively. Enormous quantities of productive power are spent on a further increase of the arsenals and on the design of new weapons which may add new, as yet unknown dangers, instead of negotiating reductions in size and stopping further research. On a few points only agreements have been concluded, and on many items many years of discussions had led nowhere.

Thirdly, these arsenals may be used because of either (i) a *regional* dispute is escalating into an uncontrollable world-wide conflict; or (ii) a pure accident creating misunderstandings and panic; or finally (iii) one of the superpowers thinks its sphere of influence is being encroached on by the other superpower.

Among the regional conflicts are those between Israel and many Arab states; the Iran–Iraq war; the Afghanistan war; the Central American conflicts; the South African conflict and wars in the Horn of Africa. There are also several slumbering conflict issues. One dangerous form they assume is terrorism.

Accidents are considered by some commentators to be potentially the most threatening. They may take the form of an error, doing something that was not intended, because of an erroneous use of a tool, by a technical defect, by a wrong interpretation of an observed movement, and so on. The equipment we are using is so complicated that many types of error are possible. And as long as errors remain possible, they will happen, with ever-increasing probability and ultimately with certainty, in the long run.

With regard to the two superpowers, both have been rigid in their views of the non-acceptability of social reform. In Eastern Europe, Czechoslovakia, Hungary and Poland have all experienced how narrow were the variations permitted by the SU. In the western hemisphere, Cuba and Nicaragua had similar experiences. In Afghanistan the SU tries to support a 'friendly' government against an indigenous guerrilla movement, as the US earlier tried unsuccessfully in Vietnam.

Many western citizens don't like and don't trust the way communist-ruled countries are run, even people who admit that in many communist-run countries a number of favourable institutions exist and operate. They don't like the monopoly of deciding how the optimal order must look, claimed by the Communist Party. In particular social democrats (democratic socialists) claim the right to hold a legitimate dissenting opinion. The way dissidents are treated in communist countries is considered to be a violation of human rights.

9.5   SUSPICION OF THE GENERAL PUBLIC: PEACE MOVEMENTS

In recent years mass movements in the West have grown in favour of arms reduction or disarmament. In Eastern Europe such movements are only possible when organised by the party or the government and spontaneous movements are suppressed. The probability is high that similar feelings do exist in Eastern Europe, however. East European governments want all peace-lovers to be communists too, but this is not necessarily the case. There is an asymmetry which should not be overlooked.

Western peace movements should be seen as an indication that the policies so far followed by all governments—communist as well as non-communist—taken together have not worked. They have only brought increased arsenals on both sides. In Western Europe the additional problem is that, like Eastern Europe, it does not want to become a war theatre. In a sense the conflict is one between the SU and the US, which tend to see the problem of the optimal social order in an over-polarised way. In this controversy both are exaggerating: neither *laissez-faire* nor complete central planning is optimal; the optimum is somewhere in between. Interestingly enough, Japan also has a mixed economy, with a greater role played by the government and more industrial democracy than the US.

The most important aspect for western countries is, of course, the security problem and in recent decades little progress has been made in this field. It is mainly this fear that is demonstrated by the mass peace movement. The solution of a complex problem should not be expected from mass demonstrations alone, however. It also requires creative thinking and the overcoming of obsolete ideas. To expect the traditional military establishments to take a leading role in the abolition of war would be as illusory as if the anti-slavery movement in the last century had expected the slave-traders and owners to take a leading role in the abolition of slavery.

As discussed before, the problem of security has been changed fundamentally by the development of nuclear weapons—or rather by weapons of the quality and in the quantities now available.

At the end of World War II, when Hiroshima and Nagasaki were bombed, the fall-out was still not such as to affect the atmosphere of the earth as a whole. So the dividing line is not qualitative, but quantitative and that quantitative frontier has now been passed.

The superpowers have more weapons than can be used, since they also hit the aggressor. Although modern polemologists (peace researchers) have used this argument, it is not certain whether they have completed their thinking.

The two superpowers are now building smaller and more accurate nuclear weapons, which they hope will not produce a 'nuclear winter' and could be used in a 'limited' way. But this may well be an illusion. Nobody can guarantee that, if nuclear weapons are ever used in a war between the superpowers their use would remain limited. That implies that nuclear weapons—and other weapons of mass destruction—do not have any real value. Only conventional weapons would have 'value'. Since the SU is stronger than the US in terms of conventional weapons in Europe it would follow that in actual fact the SU is stronger, but thinks the US is evil and stupid enough possibly to use nuclear weapons if the SU attacked—stupid, because in so doing it would commit global suicide.

Apart from these issues, the possibility of an accidental nuclear war is real and may well be the greatest danger, as already observed. Its ultimate elimination will require the dismantling of the nuclear arsenals. (Cf. also the excellent 'Background Information' by the World Council of Churches, 1986, 2: C.J. Hamelink, *Militarization in the Information Age*, Geneva.)

9.6   THE ROAD TO THE OPTIMUM; TREATIES TO BE CONFIRMED

We have now arrived at the subject proper of this chapter: the long-term East–West policy. So far we have only set the stage. Now the game must be described—not the game Alva Myrdal suspects the superpowers are playing. We must hope that a willingness to play a better game, together with the ability to play such a complicated game is forthcoming.

The real optimum, as discussed in Chapters 4, 5 and 6, is an order of common security; that is real cooperation between the superpowers. This remains a long-run goal; and not, we must hope, a mirage. But what can we propose as a road in that direction? It seems useful to discuss this topic under two headings: treaties to be confirmed and new treaties to be concluded. In this section the treaties to be confirmed will be discussed. These treaties are the (meagre) harvest from past negotiations, and it is desirable that we use them as a proof of confidence.

The three main treaties that, in our opinion, have to be confirmed are the Non-Proliferation Treaty (entered into force in 1970), the Anti-Ballistic Missile Treaty (1972) and the SALT II (signed in 1979). As is well known, the latter has not been ratified by the USA, and its numerical limits have recently been exceeded by the Reagan administration. It is desirable that compliance with the treaty be restored, as the US Senate has urged, and that it be ratified.

The crucial question remains, of course, how the existing profound mistrust between the US and the SU can be reduced. Among other methods (such as scientific, artistic and tourist cooperation in a non-political atmosphere) we think the discussions in the Standing Committee for Consultation established by Article XIII of the ABM Treaty may contribute. Such discussions are concentrating on very concrete subjects in the framework of an existing agreement. Similar occasions may be created by the conclusion of new treaties.

9.7 ADDITIONAL TREATIES TO BE CONCLUDED

Under this heading amendments or reinterpretations of already concluded treaties should be discussed.

The choice between alternative subjects and texts of treaties depends on a variety of aspects. Of these verifiability plays an important role and verifiability depends on the possibility of on-site inspection. It also depends, as we know from experience, on observation, whose technology may be improved.

The first example of an amendment to an existing treaty is the conclusion of a Comprehensive Test Ban Treaty, as an extension of the 1963 Partial Test Ban Treaty which did not apply to underground tests. The latter should also be covered.

A second example is the ban of all weapons in outer space. Here we have an example of many possible alternatives (cf. Gottfried and Lebow, 1985). These authors, after having discussed in some detail what the implications of various alternatives are, conclude that 'a comprehensive ban on the testing of space weapons and more ambitious programs to protect satellites' (p. 168) should be given preference.

A third example, and at the same time a complement to the ban just discussed, is the SU proposal made in 1981 to the UN to discuss in the GA cooperation for peaceful research of space. This proposal has not been taken up by the US, but some individual American scientists published their views in 1983 and in response the SU modified its proposals. In 1985 it was again put before the UN. The GA referred it to the CD, as stated in section 9.2.

A fourth example is a ban of all chemical weapons in an agreement that also established a Permanent Consulting Commission in order to meet regularly and adapt the agreement if circumstances make this desirable. In the report of the Palme Commission an additional proposal was made to create a chemical weapon-free zone in Europe (cf. Palme *et al.*, 1982, p. 150).

A fifth example concerns ASAT weapons. Discussions on this topic were organised by the Stockholm International Peace Research Institute (SIPRI) in September 1983, and by a symposium at UN Headquarters, convened by James Olson, Chairman of NGO Committee on Disarmament (cf. Jasani, 1985; Garwin, 1984). SIPRI recommends a complete ASAT ban as the ultimate goal, with, as a first step, a *bilateral moratorium* on testing and development of ASAT, followed by a negotiated ban on testing and an agreement on no first use of ASAT weapons.

Garwin recommends, 'in the interest of the US and international security', a treaty banning all ASAT weapons from space, all ASAT tests and use of force against space and from space to earth.

At present the SU is observing a moratorium on ASAT tests, and the US Congress has cut off all funding for ASAT tests for as long as the SU maintains its moratorium.

Last but not least, a sixth example is a group of agreements on substantial reductions in various types of armament. As mentioned in section 9.3, an elaborate proposal was made on 15 January 1986, by Secretary General Mikhael Gorbachev, containing a timetable for the elimination of all nuclear weapons by the year 2000. The necessary negotiations would be better prepared if a similar proposal were offered in response by the US or NATO, also covering the conventional supremacy of the SU.

One crucial aspect of our situation remains, of course, whether both superpowers really want to negotiate; this willingness depends on their understanding that sovereignty in matters of security does not exist.

We finish this section by mentioning that the Palme Commission lists in its report (pp. 178–81) a large number of short-term and medium-term measures, procedures for strengthening the United Nations, and regional approaches to security. Among them are proposals identical or very close to our six main examples. In this book the subject of strengthening the United Nations will be taken up in Chapter 11.

9.8 UNILATERAL STEPS

The stalemate the world is in can be broken by undertaking unilateral steps before any negotiations lead to agreements. Such unilateral steps may help to reduce the suspicion of the other party and help the world to resume a process of détente. One precondition to undertaking unilateral steps is that the level of armaments is more than is needed for the security of both sides. Although complete certainty is impossible, there are sufficient indications to initiate such a process of unilateral steps and some are practised at the time of writing such as moratoria on some programmes as an encouragement to the other party to reciprocate.

The best-known proposals on unilateral steps are those formulated by McNamara. In *Newsweek* (5 December 1983) he lists 18 short-term proposals. Some of these are for negotiations, and hence are not unilateral actions in the strict sense. But a number of others are unilateral.

...
2. Renounce the strategy of launch-on-warning.
3. Announce that we would not retaliate against a nuclear strike until we had ascertained the source of the attack, its size and the intention of the attacker (who may be a terrorist).
...
5. Renounce the strategy of decapitation strikes, that is, spare the enemy's command-and-control apparatus.
...
7. Announce immediately a policy of no first use. Publicly state that a conventional attack will be met with NATO conventional forces.
...
9. After consultation with our allies, withdraw half of our 6000 nuclear warheads now stockpiled in Western Europe.
10. Redeploy to rear areas the remaining nuclear warheads deployed along West Germany's eastern border.
...
12. Unilaterally halt the development of destabilising weapon systems and those that have no deterrent value, e.g. the neutron bomb. The MX is a destabilising system because it has a very high ratio of warheads to launchers. The Pershing II missiles are destabilising because the SU believes that they could be used for a decapitation strike.
...
14. Introduce a 'permissive action link' into every NATO warhead (electronic permission from the President).
...
16. Strengthen nuclear non-proliferation programmes, to reduce the possibility that terrorists may obtain access to nuclear warheads.
...
18. Announce a strategy of lesser retaliation—a proposal already made by McGeorge Bundy, national security advisor to Presidents Kennedy and Johnson.

9.9 NON-MILITARY POLICIES

As discussed in Part I, security is not dependent only on the use of military instruments. There is an important interconnection between instruments of economic policy and security. Helping to solve a potential opponent's economic problems, but doing so only in times of peace, may make an important contribution to both countries' security. Concrete examples are wheat exports by the US to the SU which have been a regular feature of the last decade or so. Additional examples are the supply of high-tech products that are useful only for peaceful or defensive but not for offensive activities.

In a more complicated and indirect way the opposite happened to the German Weimar Republic (1919–33). The reparation payments imposed on Germany by the Versailles Treaty of 1919 indirectly contributed to the outbreak of World War II, as discussed before and forecast by Keynes. Similarly the Japanese participation in World War II may be explained to a considerable extent by the import quotas on Japanese products between 1930 and 1941.

The results of Model C (cf. section 4.9) suggest that the impact of non-military instruments on security may be such that significant economic assistance may be part of the optimal socio-economic order.

NOTES

1. Florence Nightingale (1820–1910) was one of the leading personalities.
2. Henri Dunant (1828–1910) was the founder, who received the Nobel Peace Prize in 1901.

REFERENCES

Berkhof, G.C. (1985), 'President Reagan's S.D.I.', *Atl. Persp.* No. 2, pp. 9–16.

Chayes, A., Handler Chayes A. and Spitzer, E. (1985), 'Space Weapons the Legal Context', *Daedalus*, Summer, pp. 193–218.

Epstein, W. (1976), *The Last Chance, Nuclear Proliferation and Arms Control*, New York, The Free Press and London, Collier-Macmillan.

—— (1986), *Reviewing the Non-Proliferation Treaty*. Background Paper No. 4, Canadian Institute for International Peace and Security, Ottawa.

Garwin, R. (1984), in a Symposium Held at UN Headquarters, 26 January, *Disarmament* VII No. 2, Summer, pp. 55–82.

Gottfried, K. and Lebow, R.N. (1985), 'Anti-Satellite Weapons: Weighing the Risks', *Daedalus*, Spring, pp. 147–70.

Jasani, B. (ed.) (1985), *Space Weapons — the Arms Control Dilemma*, SIPRI, Solna, Sweden.

Kaufmann, J. (1980), *United Nations Decision Making*, Alphen aan den Rijn, The Netherlands and Rockville, MD, USA.

Keynes, J.M. (1920), *The Economic Consequences of the Peace*, London, Macmillan.

Körber-Stiftung (1985), *10 Jahre Helsinki — die Herausforderung bleibt* (10 years Helsinki — the challenge remains), Hamburg 80 (Bergedorf).

McNamara, R.S. (1983), 'What the US can do', *Newsweek*, 5 December, pp. 114–18.

Myrdal, A. (1976), *The Game of Disarmament. How the United States and Russia Run the Arms Race*, New York, Pantheon Books.

Palme, O., *et al.* (1982), *Common Security, A Blueprint for Survival*, New York, Simon and Schuster.

Sagan, Carl (1983), 'Nuclear War and Climatic Catastrophe', *Foreign Affairs* 62, No. 2, pp. 257–92.

Thorsson, I. (1981), *Disarmament, on the Verge of Failure*, Statement by Under-Secretary of State for Disarmament, Leader of the Swedish Delegation to the Committee on Disarmament, July.

Voûte, C. (1985), 'Peace and the Challenge of Space', *Colloquy on The Space Challenge for Europe*, Munich, 18–20 September, Western European Union, Assembly Committee on Scientific, Technological and Aerospace Questions.

10 Learning Processes

10.1 PEACEFUL COEXISTENCE REQUIRES LEARNING PROCESSES

Security policy as set out in Chapter 9 will only succeed if human attitudes—and in particular the attitudes of leading politicians—satisfy certain conditions. It is perfectly conceivable, unfortunately, that leading politicians do not have sufficient maturity to perform the difficult tasks they have to accomplish. In Churchill's words, we need statesmen, who unlike politicians, think of the next generation and not only of the next election. The founding fathers of the European Community were statesmen, and so was F.D. Roosevelt, to mention some western examples. In section 3.3 we dealt with human nature as a possible restriction on what can be accomplished.

The learning processes we propose to discuss here are not, of course, the learning processes by which young people acquire from the previous generation the knowledge and the insights accumulated by mankind over the centuries. Rather, the changes needed are because new circumstances prevail and discoveries have been made which were not available to the leading thinkers of the past. Adam Smith and Karl Marx were great thinkers, but nuclear energy had not been discovered in their day. Even though environmental pollution was known in London, the dimensions it would assume in the twentieth century could hardly have been imagined. We cannot blame our great thinkers of the past, but we must understand that we would be culpable if we did not take into account these discoveries or circumstances. In fact we would be behaving unscientifically if we did not integrate this new knowledge into the intellectual inheritance of humanity. Most important of all aspects of this more fundamental higher-order learning process is that we have to do it ourselves, without the help of either Adam Smith or Karl Marx. If we do not try to integrate the new insights we would be guilty of neglecting our present tasks. We can be helped in our present task by those leading scientists who were still alive or made the discovery. It remains a question of semantics whether the adapted knowledge is, or is not, called neo-liberalism or neo-Marxism. The important point is that our policies should reflect our new knowledge.

10.2 CENTRAL PROBLEMS

In an attempt to plan the higher-order learning process, let us list the central problems whose solution must be found. This is done by identifying what circumstances and discoveries essentially have affected future life and through what chains of cause and effect. Before starting this process we should remind ourselves of a fundamental defect in human beings that probably resists any attempt at learning: the ethical underdevelopment of our species. Or is it the ethical underdevelopment of the majority of political leadership? The latter possibility would still leave some hope that even here some progress is possible.

Be that as it may, by far the most influential discovery in the twentieth century was the discovery of nuclear energy. What forces led to that discovery? Contrary to many other discoveries this one was not related to ethical underdevelopment. It was curiosity and admiration for Nature. We think that all who knew Einstein, or the spirit in which fundamental physical research is done would agree. It was only some time after the possibility of tranforming matter into energy was discovered that physicists became aware of its implications. And then, very soon, ethical underdevelopment was demonstrated. Nuclear *weapons* were produced and devastated Hiroshima and Nagasaki. At the time the quantity of nuclear weapons had not yet reached the level that brought about the fundamental change in circumstances we now live in: that using nuclear weapons is suicidal. But the propensity to struggle and to use in that struggle all means available led to the military use of nuclear energy in an ever-expanding arms race and now the killing capacity available in nuclear arsenals enables the superpowers to kill all humanity.

A second change in circumstances in the twentieth century was the depletion of natural resources because of the accelerated consumption of exhaustible resources. We have already exhausted the exploitable deposits of several minerals in Europe. Many coal mines have been closed because the commercially viable deposits are exhausted. We don't have a policy to maintain the stocks available, as usual, in a rational exploitation of forests. The earth's forests are shrinking, because, for the world as a whole, we don't have a feasible policy. In addition we are destroying the quality of our trees as a consequence of acid rain. In the nineteenth century, when some of our main economic policy concepts were coined, this exhaustion of the world's resources was not taken into account.

A third example is the new technological revolution of micro-electronics. The essential features of this revolution may be formulated in different ways. One aspect of it is that the time needed to compute (that is, to find the numerical solution of a mathematical problem) has been reduced very considerably. The possibility of some technical processes depends on the speed of certain calculations. In other cases not the possibility, but the speed of a technical process depends on the speed of computations and hence productivity. In the technological revolution we are discussing computers therefore play their part. Other aspects are the replacement of manual work by machines in processes not yet mechanised and the extension of that replacement to non-manual (mental) work. This also happens with computers, but in addition there are robots, and numerically-controlled machine tools. Another catchword is automation as a wider concept than mechanisation. Finally information is involved. Information has become so much cheaper that it is introduced as a production factor in many processes where before it would not have been used. In a way the aspects mentioned are not new, but the quantities involved have risen enormously; and very large quantities may sometimes constitute a qualitative change.

The main threat resulting from this revolution is the creation of still more unemployment, partly because the precondition of employment is a level of schooling which a number of individuals are unable to complete. If the numbers of unemployed become a sizeable portion of the total population a qualitatively new phenomenon may threaten society.

Another threat of the technological revolution is the increased precision with which a missile may be launched. In certain circumstances this may create first-strike capability.

A fourth example of a phenomenon much less known a century ago is one we call counterproduction (cf. Tinbergen, 1985). This consists of a number of processes that destroy production of either the same individual or other individuals. An elementary example is vandalism. More indirect forms of counterproduction are those of pollution, already discussed. Other forms are unhealthy consumption, especially of hard drugs, but extending to more innocent forms such as sugar (rotting children's teeth) and tobacco (causing heart disease and lung cancer). As a consequence of greatly increased real income the extent of these forms of counterproduction have made them qualitatively new problems: increased counterproduction may end with self-destruction.

As a fifth and last example the new discoveries in biology should be mentioned, concerning the discovery of the structure of the very complicated molecules of which living beings are composed and of the ways in which their inherited characteristics are obtained in the process of propagation. This discovery enables man to interfere and to change the inherited properties (genetic engineering). For the time being very simple living beings only are the object of experiments, but the way seems open to extend this discovery to higher beings up to humans. The way is thus open to intervene in the spread of illnesses. Both very positive and very negative interventions are possible; one of the latter being part of biological warfare, mentioned in section 9.2.

10.3   ETHICAL UNDERDEVELOPMENT

The ethical underdevelopment of the human species manifests itself in the speed in which new discoveries of any type are being applied to harm each other by all sorts of criminal activities. Explosives found their way to murderers' guns, chemicals of many sorts were used to poison the enemy, and various types of arms races characterise the relationships between criminals and the police. This refers to micro-crime. Its counterpart, macro-crime, is the province of the military activities between nations. Technological development is very evident in this area of human activities and even pre-eminent in several types of technology. Aircraft development is a well-known example, and the penetration of nuclear energy into the military system has been mentioned many times in the preceding chapters of this book.

Ethical underdevelopment clearly showed up in the limited impact on society of the appeals to compassion for war victims made by the recipients of the Nobel Peace Prize. We mentioned earlier Henri Dunant and Bertha von Suttner. Ethical underdevelopment has also very clearly distorted religious life. The attitudes and behaviour which together constitute religious life are characterised by unbelievable inconsistencies and contradictions. Cruel wars have been fought in the name of Christianity and of other religions whose principles are love for other human beings. Policies bringing advantages to the rich were and are pursued in the name of Christ. Protestants were prosecuted and killed by Roman Catholics and vice versa in the sixteenth and seventeenth centuries and it is still happening today in Northern Ireland.

Another inconsistency is the paltry amounts made available by the 'Christian' West for development assistance.

10.4 SOURCES OF LEARNING: THEORY

Learning essentially springs from two main sources, and preferably simultaneously from both. We shall call them *theory* and *experience*. By learning from theory we mean learning from thinking about the relationships between two or more variables, e.g. aims and means of policy. Here policy stands for human action in order to attain certain objectives or aims and means are a specification of that action. The concepts of aims and means have been discussed extensively in Chapters 1–4. In fact, the object of publishing the present book is to set in motion a learning process by the reader, after the authors have themselves gone through many learning processes. This implies, *inter alia*, that our opinions after completing this book differ from the opinions we held before starting to write it. They don't differ on all points we are trying to make, but they do on some points.

Scientific thinking is a complex activity, composed of many elements. These elements may be relationships between the entities, phenomena or variables with which some science—the science we are thinking about—is concerned. The most important science for this book may be called peace research, or, more exactly, the economics of peace research; or generalised economics. The generalisation consists of the integration into economics of security as an aim alongside the traditional aims of applied economics.

We use the term 'peace research' because it has become a concept inspiring confidence in present generations. The learning process this chapter deals with may be defined as adapting one's ideas about socio-economic policy to the results of peace research.

As one of the central examples we quote the proposition derived from peace research that a nuclear war cannot be won. If this proposition is integrated into existing theories of how to settle international conflicts, it will considerably change these theories.

Another example of how existing theories of socio-economic policy may be changed by the results of peace research is the change in theories which have so far neglected the impact of war on human welfare. The much stronger impact of modern (even non-nuclear) war on human welfare may make such neglect impossible, or the theory will be seen to be utterly unrealistic.

A third example may be taken from the theory of the optimum level of decision-making (cf. section 5.4). The application of this theory to the problem of how to attain an unpolluted planet teaches us that nations have to give up sovereignty in matters of environmental policy. Once there is agreement on this issue the question may be raised whether national sovereignty on other decisions has to be given up.

10.5 SOURCES OF LEARNING: EXPERIENCE

The other source from which we can learn is by experience. Many people attach even more importance to what they have learned from experience than to what theories might teach them: they have a healthy suspicion of theories. Perhaps they overlook that their own interpretation of their experience constitutes a theory; but we can all agree that facts are harder evidence than doctrines. Wars are facts and hard evidence in more than one sense. They, and their impact on human life, have been engraved on many people's lives so deeply that they will never be forgotten. If common themes in the conduct of wars have been observed by individuals accustomed to think, this may have brought about a learning process. To the majority of world citizens theories are not interesting, but their experience and the experience of people they trust are far more persuasive.

One central tendency in the history of wars is that in previous centuries wars were fought between neighbouring political units and that these units were for the most part much smaller than the political units we now know. Many of today's nations are the result of an integration of smaller units that were sovereign in earlier centuries. Obvious examples among today's medium-sized nations are Germany and Italy. Both these countries became one unit somewhat more than a century ago, around

1870. Britain and France had become units earlier. But the traces of smaller units can easily be found in geographical subdivisions, such as counties. Even a small country like the Netherlands until 1648 consisted of counties, duchies, etc. And these smaller units were at war with one another often enough. So there is considerable evidence that, by and large, we now have larger units, composed of what previously were smaller sovereign units.

There are exceptions of course. In Europe, an important exception is the history of the 'double monarchy' Austria-Hungary, which consisted not only of Austria and Hungary, but also of large parts of today's Czechoslovakia, parts of Poland, Italy, Romania and smaller parts of Yugoslavia. A partly European exception is the British Commonwealth. The process of integration had taken place under colonialism, partly within Europe (Wales, Scotland, Ireland), but largely over all continents. Here the process of disintegration started with the separation of the present Irish republic, gained momentum after World War I and was accelerated after World War II. Similar developments took place in the French colonial empire, but are not expected to happen in European France.

The superpowers experienced integration and as yet no sign of disintegration. After the American Civil War (1861–65) the integration became stronger and now wars between American states are extremely unlikely. The same seems to be true for the Soviet Union.

The overall picture seems strongly to support the experience that integration has been a potent force banning war as a means of settling conflicts between previously sovereign units, in particular when that integration was voluntary and desired. So much so that voluntary integration might well be one of the most reliable means to end war.

10.6   WHAT WOULD WORLD WAR III LOOK LIKE?

A useful part of a learning process directed at reshaping established policies is an attempt to forecast the qualitative and quantitative features of a third world war. A number of such attempts have been made. In doing so one must avoid the well-known error made in the past by both military and civilian authorities. The error consists of preparing to refight the last war. Military authorities have been accused repeatedly of doing so, for the obvious reason—not unfamiliar to many scientists—

that they want to work with reliable data. Obviously the data they use are from the last war. In the Netherlands once a month we check whether the air raid warnings still operate. One study (Siccama, 1984) wonders whether the general public does not even look back to World War I when trying to imagine what World War III would be like. But even a conventional war fought with today's weapons would be extremely destructive. Siccama points out that many have failed to recognise this.

Here we are at the heart of our question. Any attempt to forecast the qualitative and quantitative features of World War III must superimpose on the data about World War II the developments that have occurred in the meantime with regard to weapons already available in 1939 and to the new weapons since developed. On various occasions we have quoted that the destructive capacity of the nuclear arsenal now available is about five times what is needed to kill the world population (Röling, 1985). As an illustration of what nuclear war would mean a simple statement by the organisation 'International Physicians for the Prevention of Nuclear War' (Nobel Peace Prize winners in 1985) that practically no medical assistance would be available to the millions seriously wounded is more convincing than any figure. So are the statements about 'nuclear winter', made by the US National Academy of Sciences and by Professor Sergei Kapitza of the Moscow Physio-Technical Institute and the Institute for Physical Problems, Soviet Academy of Sciences (cf. US National Academy of Sciences, quoted by Disarmament, a periodic review by the UN, Spring 1985; and S. Kapitza, quoted in the same review, Spring 1985). According to a US National Academy report, temperature around the centres attacked, between 40° and 70° northern latitude except near the coasts, may fall 10°–25°C below normal in summer for at least a few weeks. This report contains many more particulars and is careful in setting out a large number of uncertainties.

Professor Kapitza gives historical evidence about well-known volcanic explosions, in particular of Mountain Tambora (1815)— one of the consequences was that 1816 was known, in the moderate Northern hemisphere, as the 'year without a summer'.

A third way of characterising World War III may consist of rereading what happened in Hiroshima and Nagasaki in 1945 and keeping in mind that the explosive capacity of today's stockpile of arms corresponds to approximately 1,600,000 Hiroshima bombs.

10.7   WHO HAS TO LEARN WHAT?

We pointed out that the environment humanity is living in, as a consequence of unforeseen developments and new discoveries, unknown one or two centuries ago, requires a learning process in order to adapt our views on welfare and security and the policies to maximise them. For these are usually based on the opinions of leading scholars of the past who could not envisage the present environment. We reminded our readers of the necessity to think about the adaptations ourselves, and our responsibilities in this respect. It seems desirable to be more explicit in setting out these responsibilities. Obviously leading people of various sorts are more involved than others, but in democracies (whether 'parliamentary' or 'people's') some responsibility rests upon the citizens' shoulders as well.

In the present section we shall discuss more explicitly five types of leading personalities and deal more specifically with the lessons they have to learn or to try to learn. If the present leaders are not able to learn, the people must choose new leaders, or force the 'leaders' to follow them.

The first category we consider are *government* leaders; and in particular the leaders of governments of powerful nations. Important subjects for them to think over are the limits to sovereignty and the benefits of integration. The first subject was discussed in section 4.9; the second will be discussed in more detail in Chapter 12.

The second category we consider will be the leaders of political parties. Of course, there is considerable overlap with the first group and in parliamentary democracies (which we consider to be true democracies) the same persons can alternatively be part of the first and part of the second group. Leaders of a political party are supposed to check the policies actually pursued with the principles they stand for. This constitutes a more penetrating thinking process than required in daily practice. It will be desirable for them too to think about the limits to sovereignty and the usefulness of integration. In addition they may try to delve more deeply. Our recommendations are to give thought to the dangers of polarisation—the tendency to defend extremist ideas—and the importance of tolerance. Coexistence does require some forms of tolerance. Other topics are how to react *vis-à-vis* vandalism and other sorts of counterproduction, including corruption, theft, unhealthy consumption, and so on. Recommendations of the kind we are now discussing are always needed more by extremists than by leaders at the centre. Extremists often expect more from rigid principles than others. Are not communists and ultra-liberalists both interested above all in spreading their principles? Let them not forget that their ideals cease making sense in a nuclear war-stricken world and that, therefore, to keep the world at peace is a precondition to what they once thought was their primary task, spreading their principles. The latter will not make sense if that precondition is not fulfilled first.

The third category of leading personalities we want to consider are trade union leaders. One of the lessons they have to learn is the importance of reducing unemployment. In the past they often gave more attention to the welfare of their working members than to that of unemployed. The impact of unemployment on people is psychologically much more devastating than is often believed (cf. Pelzmann, 1985).

It should be clear that not only trade union leaders, but also government, party and employers' federation leaders, should be aware of the need to reduce unemployment.

Employers' leaders are the fourth group we shall consider. Alongside reducing unemployment, their relation to governments touches upon their immediate responsibilities. They should understand, in particular, that not only within nations, but also outside them some public regulation is necessary. It is a general truth that the law-abiding will gain from some regulation, and without it they may themselves be the victims of the non-law-abiding. It is also true that regulation may degenerate into bureaucracy if pushed too far.

The fifth group we want to consider are, of course, military leaders. We have already mentioned one possible error they are accused of, namely the tendency to base their projections of the future on the last war's experience; and they are not the only ones to do so. The most difficult lesson they have to learn is to understand the purpose of nuclear weapons. There is a dawning understanding that the purpose is not to use them. There is less understanding for the conclusion that, in the end, this role should extend to not manufacturing them either. Another conclusion, namely that the best organisation of world security is to cooperate with the enemies in order to establish that security, is the indispensable missing link. The military leaders' problem may perhaps be formulated in the most challenging way by asking: who will be the first to take the decisive step towards organised world security—the governments, the military, or another group?

REFERENCES

Kapitza, S. (1985), 'Global consequences of a nuclear war and the world after', *Disarmament* VIII, No. 1, pp. 121–31. (United Nations).

Pelzmann, L. (1985), *Wirtschaftspsychologie*, Arbeitslosenforschung, Schattenwirtschaft, Steuerpsychologie, Wien and New York, Springer.

Röling, B.V.A. (1985), personal correspondence.

Siccama, J.G. (1984), 'De voorlaatste oorlog overdoen?' (Re-running the last war but one?), *Internationale Spectator* 38, pp. 445–8.

Tinbergen, J. (1985), *Production, Income and Welfare*, Brighton, Wheatsheaf Books, Chapter 4, pp. 35–42.

United States National Academy of Sciences, Report of (1985), *Disarmament* VIII, No. 1, pp. 110–20.

11 Strengthening the United Nations

11.1 THE EXISTING STRUCTURE OF THE UNITED NATIONS; ITS PERFORMANCE

In this chapter we propose to discuss how the family of United Nations (UN) institutions must be reformed if an optimum management of our planet ('The Earth, Inc.') is considered to be its task. Again we admit that this is an ambitious task, and presumably not the task the original organisers had in mind. Presumably they were not fully aware of what the problems in the mid–1980s, forty years after the creation of the UN, would be. Some of the greatest problems were already apparent, though: the end of the alliance between the US and the SU, and the use of *nuclear weapons* against Hiroshima and Nagasaki.

What we propose here is not the most likely development of the United Nations institutions, nor even the politically feasible development, and still less what the present governments of most countries and in particular those of the superpowers probably prefer. The subject is, rather, a sketch of the structure *needed* to attain an optimal management.

It seems appropriate first to remind the reader of what institutions the family consists of; to give some information about the financing of these institutions, and to summarise the principal actions of these institutions.

Table 11.1 presents the institutions in alphabetical order of the acronyms used to indicate them, the full name and the location.

It is clear that in many very diversified fields the need for international cooperation exists, reflecting the numerous ways in which the world's economies are interwoven. Given the aversion to international intervention, we can safely assume that the real need for such intervention surpasses the present extent.

Table 11.1 Family of United Nations institutions

FAO	Food and Agriculture Organisation	Rome
GATT	General Agreement on Tariffs and Trade	Geneva
IAEA	International Atomic Energy Agency	Vienna
ICAO	International Civil Aviation Organisation	Montreal
ICJ	International Court of Justice	The Hague
IFAD	International Fund for Agricultural Development	Rome
ILO	International Labour Organisation	Geneva
IMF	International Monetary Fund	Washington, D.C.
IMO	International Maritime Organisation	London
ITU	International Telecommunications Union	Geneva
UNCTAD	United Nations Conference on Trade and Development	Geneva
UNCTC	United Nations Centre for Transnational Corporations	New York
UNDP	United Nations Development Programme	New York
UNDRO	United Nations Disaster Relief Office	Geneva
UNEP	United Nations Environmental Programme	Nairobi
UNESCO	United Nations Educational, Scientific and Cultural Organisation.	Paris
UNFPA	United Nations Fund for Population Activities	New York
UNHCR	United Nations High Commissioner for Refugees	New York
UNHQ	United Nations Head Quarters (Secretariat)	New York
UNICEF	United Nations Children Fund	New York
UNIDIR	United Nations Institute for Disarmament Reseach	Geneva
UNIDO	United Nations Industrial Development Organisation	Vienna
UNITAR	United Nations Institute for Training and Research	New York
UNRISD	United Nations Research Institute for Social Development	Geneva
UNRWA	United Nations Relief and Works Agency for Palestine Refugees	New York
UNA	United Nations University	Tokyo
UPU	Universal Postal Union	Berne
WBG	World Bank Group*	Washington, D.C.
WHO	World Health Organisation	Geneva
WIDER	World Institute for Development Economics Research	Helsinki
WIPO	World Intellectual Property Organisation	Geneva
WMO	World Meteorological Organisation	Geneva

* Composed of World Bank (WB), International Finance Corporation (IFC) and International Development Association (IDA).

The total contributions to the United Nations institutions (excluding IMF and WBG), are of the order of \$5000 million (5×10^9); world income, as estimated by Kravis *et al.* (1982, p. 344), amounts to \$10 billion (10^{13}) for 1977 and probably not much more for 1982; hence about 1/2 per mille of world income is spent on what should become the world's federal government. In a well-organised nation such as the US it amounts to c. 20 per cent. Whereas for the world at large a clearly lower percentage would be optimal, in all likelihood the figure of less than 1/2 per mille is too low.

Be that as it may, the contributions made by various member nations are astonishingly different. Although the US contributes about \$1.3 thousand million (10^9), which is more than any other country, this is *per capita* of its population \$5.74 (1984); countries such as Norway and Sweden contribute several times this amount. (Data can be found in the 33rd Annual Report 'United States Contributions to International Organisations' (Department of State Publication 9452).)

On the 40th anniversary of the United Nations (although not of all its institutions) many commentators surveyed what had been accomplished during this period. Such a survey may be a useful starting point for an evaluation and possibly for reforms. As one of the constructive commentators the Stanley Foundation may be quoted for a clear and balanced survey (Stanley Foundation, 1985), based on a three-day conference in which fifteen UN diplomats, scholars and Secretariat officials participated. Among the accomplishments the group mentions decolonisation, which raised the number of member nations threefold in forty years—a process that had been expected to take a century. Of course many forces were at work to accelerate this process, but at least one undesirable type of relationship between nations was eliminated almost entirely.

The creation of international law is considered by the group to be another significant and positive activity. The International Court of Justice was created and some 20,000 treaties have been concluded.

The United Nations has also fostered global behavioural norms. War is no longer glorified. The UN Environmental Programme has set standards for the global environment.

Even so, unfortunately, the report informs us that during the last forty years 150 wars, resulting in 20 million deaths, have taken place. In 107 other cases (according to a study up to 1968) the UN succeeded in halting a war or averting a potential conflict.

To these findings of the Stanley Foundation conference (recorded here only in part) we may add that the main performance of the UN institutions consists in producing large quantities of information and an enormous volume of recommendations for economic development. Extensive studies have been made of many of the new problems the world faces, the population 'explosion', pollution, desertification, soil erosion, deforestation, and the threat of nuclear war. An impressive number of annual and occasional publications has been made available.

In an evaluation of the UN contribution to a better world management our conclusion can only be, however, that little has been accomplished. Perhaps we should add that 'life begins at forty'. We should also point out that it is more the behaviour of member nations that is to blame than the contribution of the United Nations. It is unfair to hold the UN responsible for not having been able to prevent all wars. At least the UN never started a war, unlike many of its members.

11.2   THE NEED TO STRENGTHEN THE UNITED NATIONS; REFORMS AND EXISTING INSTITUTIONS

Our aim is to outline how the United Nations institutions might be transformed into a system of world management. We don't deny that other roads to such a system are conceivable; but we do submit that transforming the UN is preferable. That transformation may profit from the experience of well-run national governments as well as from experience of transnational enterprises, trade unions and political parties; again experience of the best-run among them. In our attempt we shall draw heavily on the reports of some independent international commissions (Brandt, Palme, and their predecessors).

The main theme will be dealt with under two headings: the transformation of existing institutions and the creation of additional institutions. The former subject is dealt with in this section and sections 11.3–11.6, the latter subject in section 11.7. Some of our proposals were announced in Chapter 7.

One of the main reasons why the United Nations is not seen as an agency to be respected by the large and powerful nations results from the way in which its members are represented in the General Assembly—one vote per member (the IMF and the WBG are organised differently). The number of votes a nation is entitled to should depend on the size of its population and the size of its financial contribution. The first is a question of democracy and the latter corresponds to the stage of development towards democracy the world has attained. It is somewhat optimistic to believe that the stage the world at large has reached corresponds with the stage in the developed countries when only those had voting rights who paid taxes or a similar representation of their incomes. Voting rights for all were only introduced after World War I.

The second reason why the United Nations decisions are not respected may be the difference between the span of control in a business management structure and the 'span of control' of the UN Secretary General if we consider him as the potential 'Chief Executive' of World Management.

One reform we would recommend for study is one where the world's main strategy is decided upon in a meeting of some twelve to fifteen authoritative representatives of the five to ten most powerful nations or federations, while the remaining 100 or so nations would be represented by other new federations (cf. also section 5.4).

The most powerful nations are already federations: this applies to the two superpowers, to India and to Brazil; only China and Japan are more centralised.

Some of the regions not yet mentioned which may conceivably be interested in establishing a sufficiently large federation are the Spanish speaking Latin-American nations, with an integrated Central American–Caribbean unit, and the 'Arab nation'. In some other areas, such as ASEAN and black Africa, cooperative schemes exist that might serve as nuclei.

The subject for study we formulated was inspired by a business management structure. An alternative is to consider a national government structure as the source of inspiration. The Executive then may have a 'span of control' of up to 1000 'Members of Parliament' (or a few hundred Senators) where the number of members depends on the size and financial contributions of the nations represented. For the most powerful nations this alternative is less attractive, since their size cannot then be reflected in the number of representatives they have: the very small countries will still have one representative, not one-half or one-tenth of a person. Also in this alternative there is no built-in incentive for small countries to enter into a federation of more members, as in the first alternative. To remedy that situation representatives from very small nations might have to be given a lower voting weight.

In the present section all UN institutions in need of reform will be discussed (except the four most important ones which will be discussed in sections 11.3–11.6 inclusive). For our purpose some of these are less important, because they refer to institutions which already operate relatively satisfactorily. This applies in particular to the 'Bretton Woods institutions', the IMF and WBG. Their operation gives rise to partly opposite proposals for reform. Whereas the UN Development Planning Committee, in its 40th report, suggests that IMF's consultation and surveillance should be strengthened (p. 2), the opposite complaint formulated by Taylor (1984), also makes sense, namely that IMF lending conditions aim at a deflationary process. When applied to a large number of debtor countries this may produce a new recession. In a sense the debtor countries are burdened with the full amount of the total debt, partly caused by the donor countries which never lived up to the recommendations of the Pearson Commission and all its successors.[1]

This is the reason why the developing countries have long proposed that they should be represented more adequately on the boards of both IMF and WBG. In terms of parliamentary history this means that a step in the direction of full democracy be set.

For both Bretton Woods institutions we follow the Brandt Commission in proposing that more means be made available to them. Of course this is less a reform than a fuller operation; it is a 'reform' of the donor countries. Here too we have the UN Development Planning Commission on our side (40th Report, p. 3).

The last reform to be discussed in this section deals with matters of international trade. Here again the UN Planning Commission is quite explicit. Less protection is advocated on pages 9 and 11, including the elimination (p. 14) of import impediments to textiles. The Leutwiler Report to GATT is followed, recommending a timetable to attain its recommendations. We think that in particular the Multifibre Agreement, restricting textile imports into developed countries, should be discontinued. Textile and clothing industries have had enough time to reorganise. The dynamic enterprises among them did so years ago.

11.3   STRENGTHENING OF THE UN SECURITY COUNCIL

Of all tasks entrusted to the United Nations that of maintaining peace is the most important. Within the UN structure the responsibility for peacekeeping rests with the Security Council. Present procedures of that Council are paralysed, however, by the veto power of the permanent members. This reflects, of course, the lack of consensus among these members and, in particular, the fact that they are not prepared to transfer their sovereignty in matters of peace and war to the Security Council. In addition, the Security Council does not have the power to implement its decision. Reforms of the Council are, therefore, necessary if we want to take these tasks seriously.

Moreover, we must be aware of the complementarity of the Security Council's task and that of the Court of Justice. (The latter will be dealt with in the next section.) This complementarity becomes clear immediately if we consider the positive alternative to war: *peaceful change.* Peacekeeping must not be used as an argument in favour of maintaining the status quo, that is of conservatism. The world community is and must be a vital institution, adapting itself to new ideas, if these are better than existing ideas, eliminating inequities resulting from unjustified power. Hence the world's institutions must be such that necessary change can take place: peaceful change must be possible. If ways of eliminating unemployment are discovered and have been tested, their application must not be blocked by simple conservatism. If the world's resources are distributed highly unevenly ways and means must be made available to redress—to satisfy world public opinion—that distribution.

The proposals for reforming the UN Security Council we submit here have partly been derived from the Palme Report's proposals, especially those referring to 'strengthening the UN security system' (Palme *et al.* 1982, pp. 161–77). These are intended to achieve a more satisfactory execution of Article 99 of the UN Charter, which authorises the Secretary-General 'to bring to the attention of the Security Council any matter which in his opinion may threaten the maintenance of international peace and security'. The Palme Commission recommends 'the implementation of a modified version of the UN Charter's concept of collective security. Its basis would be political agreement and partnership between the permanent members of the Security Council and the Third World' (p. 162). In the

Commission's opinion such an agreement is a prerequisite for the effective functioning of the UN in maintaining international peace and security (p. 163).

We believe that this is one alternative of many. One essential element is that the two superpowers must be included. Their agreement remains the most important and the most difficult to attain. They may be accompanied by their NATO and Warsaw Pact allies, or by the EEC and the CMEA (Comecon) and Third World representatives. The agreement might be negotiated in two steps—first by the superpowers and subsequently with others: Europeans in one or another grouping and Third World representatives. The Palme Commission will have had good reasons for their recommendation; accordingly our main additional suggestion is to negotiate in two steps.

The driving forces needed to reach an agreement need hardly be repeated: it is far-sighted self-interest. It must be hoped that no short-sighted propensity to retain sovereignty will block an agreement. The World Federalist proposal (as applied, for instance, in the Federal Republic of Germany) that each nation transfers its sovereignty in the use of military forces to the Security Council is a promising suggestion.

A complement to a more powerful Security Council is a Police Force. Some modest experiences have been gained with the United Nations peace force in maintaining peace in areas where conflicts existed between small and hence non-powerful nations. The creation of a peace or police force for the world at large constitutes a new and crucial problem which will be outlined in section 11.8.

11.4　THE ROLE OF THE INTERNATIONAL COURT OF JUSTICE

The role of the International Court of Justice is, in principle, complementary to that of the Security Council. The relationship may be clarified by reminding ourselves of the role of wars in the past, before they had become impossible, and by introducing the concept of a *just war*. Such wars were accepted as a means to change international structures if no other ways could be found to eliminate injustice. As examples we may mention the occupation of one country by a more powerful one (i.e. colonialism), the exclusion of one country from international trade (e.g. the situation in which Japan found itself in 1941), or a country with limited access to world oceans (one of the problems of Russia). The reader will easily think of many other examples: there is no denying the existence of inequities in the distribution across nations of basic resources.

As we observed in the preceding section, the Security Council's task is to prevent warfare, since warfare is inhumane and nuclear warfare presages the end of civilisation. But this is not the solution to the problem that gives rise to the threat of a just war, that is, if an inequitable structural element of the world order has to be eliminated. Here the important task of a fully developed International Court of Justice starts. It is the Court which, ideally, must be asked (i) to judge whether there is an inequitable structural element and (ii) by what change equity will be served.

In cases where international law is applicable the Court's procedure will be legally determined. In the many cases where such law does not exist, the Court will find challenges to create new international law.

An interesting large-scale and novel example where the world is close to an expansion of international law is the Law of the Sea (Mann Borgese, 1982, 1985). This will be discussed in the next section.

11.5   LAW OF THE SEA — TO BE FOLLOWED BY A LAW OF SPACE?

The draft Law of the Sea drawn up after nine years of negotiation (cf. section 5.7) is an example of the adaptation to new discoveries and theories about the optimal socio-economic order which we discussed in Chapter 10. The draft was signed by the representatives of the US, UK and West German governments in power at the time but have not been ratified by the present governments. The short-term interests of national business are given greater weight by the present governments.

As the US Conference of Catholic Bishops (1983) stressed, leaving the allocation of ocean resources to a power struggle will simply insure the emergence of new conflicts in the future.

Since the new draft Law of the Sea constitutes a masterpiece of inventiveness and imaginative new principles, and because of the similarities between the planet's oceans and the space around the planet, the question may be asked whether a similar procedure could not be applied for dealing with the optimal use of space—

the subject on which the Soviet Union made a proposal in the 1985 General Assembly of the United Nations. This proposal was submitted in the form of a draft resolution proposing an examination of 'the possiblity of convening ... an international conference with the participation of states with major capabilities and of other interested states to consider ... international cooperation in the peaceful exploration and use of outer space ... including ... the setting up of a world space organisation.'

The General Assembly referred the subject to the Conference of Disarmament to report to the Assembly at its 41st (1987) session and decided to include in the provisional agenda of that session: 'Prevention of an arms race in outer space.'

11.6   UNITED NATIONS ENVIRONMENTAL PROGRAMME

This programme is the UN institution in charge of the collection of data and the recommending policies to attain and maintain a clean environment. Established after the Stockholm conference of 1972 and located in Nairobi, UNEP published a report *The World Environment, 1972–1982*, edited by M.W. Holdgate *et al.* (1982) which provides us with a wealth of data on the state of the environment and its trends, as far as information permits. A warming of the earth's climate could not be reported with certainty, and on deforestation conflicting evidence was presented, but it was clear that the world's environmental system constitutes essentially a unity and that the possibility of a future 'greenhouse effect' due to the increase of atmospheric carbon dioxide (CO_2) has to be taken seriously, as has the damage caused by acid rain. In 1980 the creation of CO_2 by burning fossil fuels amounted to 10 per cent of the quantity used by green plants in photosynthesis. Urban air pollution in underdeveloped countries had become comparable to earlier air pollution in cities of the developed countries: Calcutta in 1980 was like London in 1952/53. Technologies to cope with environmental problems in developed countries have been developed and total costs to clean and maintain the environment estimated at a few per cent of national incomes. People now understand the problem and the need to solve it, but the time has come to implement these solutions. Within single countries many projects have been executed and in Europe international cooperation had been given high priority. It is uncertain whether governments everywhere and existing organisations are able to carry out the necessary programmes.

Five years after the data on which the report was drafted several of the threats have become more evident, especially deforestation by acid rain and uncontrolled wood felling for various purposes. The urgent need for coordinated policies is now clear. This requires, as in other cases discussed, the competence of UNEP to make policy decisions and power to implement them. Although some problems (for instance, the pollution of rivers and lakes) may be dealt with by continental or regional organisations, world-wide supervision will be needed even here if rivers are cleaned insufficiently and the pollution of the oceans worsens. World-wide action will be needed anyway to halt atmospheric pollution and pollution of the oceans by oil-tankers, for which a responsible ocean authority will have to be created.

Alongside the known threats other, unknown threats to forests have developed whose causes are not yet understood.

With the necessity for the UNEP to have a firmer grip on the world's nations a more reasonable system of representation of the member nations, as discussed in section 11.2, becomes more urgent as well.

11.7 CREATION OF ADDITIONAL UN INSTITUTIONS; A WORLD TREASURY

In the preceding section we saw that awareness of environmental pollution has made it necessary to set up a new institution, UNEP, to the family of UN institutions. In section 11.5 we also discussed a new institution, a space agency. Evidently we must remain prepared, as observed in Chapter 10, to adapt our political ideals and programmes to new developments in technology and new inventions.

One such discovery might be that in well-organised lower entities—in this case well-organised nations—institutions exist which do not exist at the world level, that is, in the UN system. Within a well-organised country there are usually three financial institutions: a central bank, an investment bank and a Treasury (or Ministry of Finance). In the United Nations system the IMF is comparable but not identical to the central bank and it is desirable that it develops further in that direction. Similarly the World Bank Group is almost identical to an investment bank.

But in the United Nations system we don't find anything comparable to a Treasury. Each institution has its own Treasury and there is little coordination, in contradistinction to the important and central role of Treasuries in autonomous and well-run countries (cf. section 7.2).

This may serve as a justification of our proposal in section 7.2 to add to the UN family of institutions a World Treasury (WT) and to combine this with some proposals on how it should operate. The essential characteristic of a Treasury is that it deals with current expenditures and current revenue. Part of these current expenditures are spent on current tasks such as the operation of the UN institutions which now have their own budgets. This would introduce the possibility of *priority-setting*. The other part of current expenditures is spent on investments and will be booked, perhaps, on a capital account. The advantage of financing investments out of a current budget, instead of from loans, is considerable. There is no need to negotiate a repayment scheme and the interest to be paid, with the country in which the investment takes place because no debt is created. This also implies that renegotiation in case of overindebtedness—one of our present difficulties—is superfluous.

On the revenue side a Treasury levies taxes and this implies that a system of contributing to the UN budget takes the place of voluntary contributions—or rather of voluntary non-contributions. Contributions should be legally defined and not depend on changes in governments; this is the rule inside well-organised national economies and would contribute a qualitative improvement of the operation of the UN.

Among the more specialised new agencies that have been proposed recently is the Satellite Monitoring Agency, proposed by France in 1978 and still worth being reconsidered. Perhaps it could become part of the proposal for an Agency of Peaceful Research of Space, proposed in 1985 by the Soviet Union (cf. section 11.5).

11.8   CREATION OF ADDITIONAL UN INSTITUTIONS; A POLICE FORCE

As observed at the end of section 11.3, this constitutes a new and extremely difficult problem, crucial to the attainment of joint security but hardly discussed so far. The Palme Report has little to say about this subject.

The necessity for a UN Police Force may, as for other institutions, be based, first of all, on the comparison with well-organised countries. Maintenance of law and order in every country and at all times requires an armed police force. The level of armament will be the lower the higher the existing cohesion in the country. For the world at large that cohesion is weak and hence a rather high level of police armament will be necessary in the beginning.

The necessity of a UN Police Force may also be argued more directly; in the early phases of negotiations about new forms of coexistence—for instance, by taking Secretary-General Gorbachev's proposals for disarmament as the starting point—there is a real danger of divergence between the level of armaments each of the two superpowers will maintain officially and the level it will maintain in reality. Let us call the party behaving in such a way the 'Supposed Deviant Power'. Both superpowers will think it is the other.

The UN Police Force must be a neutralising element, able to offset the secret armaments.

The strength of the Police Force must discourage the offensive use of the secret arms. If it is assumed that an offensive use will be successful with 100 per cent probability only if it is three times as strong as the opposing force, the UN Police Force should have a strength of one third of the likely secret forces of the Supposed Deviant Power.

An idea of the latter's forces may be derived from the deviations between the estimates of both superpowers as discussed in Vienna, or on previous occasions where missile gaps were supposed to exist. Certain limits are set to these deviations by the availability of 'national technical means of verification', otherwise known as spying with the aid of aircraft or satellites.

The Police Force should not consist of American or Soviet forces, since their forces cannot be supposed to resist their own compatriots.

Care must of course be taken that the World Police Force is not abused by any small group to serve its special interest, but carries out the decisions of the (reformed) Security Council, which must defend global justice and serve the interest of the entire world population.

NOTE

1. The total debt of the developing countries is about the same as the amount that the official development assistance fell short, in the last decade, as recommended by the Pearson and Brandt Commissions.

REFERENCES

Committee for Development Planning of the UN (1985), 40th annual report: *The Challenge to Multilateralism. A Time for Renewal*, United Nations, New York.

Holdgate, M.W. *et al.* (eds) (1982), *The World Environment 1972–1982. A report by UNEP*, Dublin, Tycooly International Publishing.

Kravis, I.B. *et al.* (1982), *World Product and Income*, World Bank, Baltimore and London, The Johns Hopkins University Press.

Mann Borgese, E. (1982), 'The Law of the Sea: the Next Phase', *Third World Quarterly* 4, No. 4, 692–718.

—— (1985), *The Mines of Neptune*, New York, Harry N. Abrams, Inc., especially Chapter 6.

Palme, O. *et al.* (1982), *Common Security. A Blueprint for Survival*, New York, Simon and Schuster.

Stanley Foundation (1985), *The First Forty Years*, Muskatine, IA.

Taylor, L. (1984), 'IMF Conditionality: incomplete theory, policy malpractice', in *Middle East Technical University, Studies in Development*, Nos 1 and 2, Ankara, Middle East Technical University.

US Conference of Catholic Bishops (1983), 'Pastoral Letter on War, Armaments and Peace', *Origins* 13, No. 1.

12 Integration as a Strategy

12.1 INTEGRATION AS A MEANS TO END WAR

As pointed out in section 10.4, experience has shown that integration of small sovereign areas into larger ones has been an effective way to end war. In the present chapter a number of past and present processes of integration will be discussed in order to understand to what use this process can be put in the future in order to end war, hence become an instrument to end war. In contradistinction to the problem of how best to manage the planet integration is a process often operating from the 'grass roots' (or below) to the 'summit' (or upward). Here the citizens can be the actors. Citizens are motivated by two opposing forces, (integration versus disintegration, or cooperation versus repulsion). Cooperation is often the answer to a common danger; repulsion the answer to a need to 'find one's own identity'. Countries occupied by a powerful nation unite in order to liberate themselves. Within a country a group with their own language or religion wants to obtain independence (secession) or at least some degree of autonomy. The (Protestant) Netherlands, from 1568 to 1648, fought their Eighty-Year War to liberate themselves from (Catholic) Spain; the thirteen American colonies fought their liberation war against England and so on. Both forces were at work in these examples: the Dutch provinces integrated themselves to become the United Provinces; the American colonies became the United States, in order to separate themselves from Spain, respectively England. In the following sections we shall consider a number of examples in a more systematic way: distinguishing past integration processes from current processes, in order to learn how in the future to promote integration as a policy to end war. We shall also consider separately the superpowers, the medium-size present-day powers in Europe, as well as some of the small countries, and, for comparison, some Asian countries. The emphasis in all our examples will be on the countries' present-day structure. We shall discover many similarities in the structures of integrated countries.

Finally, there are also comparisons to be made and similarities to be discovered at various levels of integration within the same hierarchy. Thus, Scharpf (1985) compares the structure of the Federal Republic of Germany with the structure of the European Community, which is one level higher within the European Community hierarchy. Such comparisons can be made, of course, in many hierarchies and open up promising perspectives for more fundamental research. The phenomenon studied in particular by Scharpf is the joint decision about a problem by two successive hierarchical levels, which he calls 'policy intertwining'. This sort of common decision by two successive levels means a type of weighted voting. Let the levels be the federal government and one particular *Land*, then the interests of the latter are represented twice and those of the other *Länder* once. The question may then be asked whether these weights coincide with the impact of the problem treated on the welfare of the two types of *Länder*.

The idea that European integration is able to contribute to world integration has been set out convincingly by Chr. Layton in the report 'One Europe: one World', written in conjunction with a group sponsored by the Federal Trust for Education and Research, the Wyndham Place Trust and the One World Trust, 1986.

12.2   EXAMPLES OF COMPLETED INTEGRATION: THE SUPERPOWERS

Both superpowers, the SU and the US, are federative hierarchies. The Soviet Union in many respects can be seen as the successor of the Tsarist Russian Empire, whose territory included an enormous Asian territory, Siberia, colonised in previous centuries. The Tsarist territory also included, until 1917, Finland, the Baltic states (Lithuania, Latvia and Estonia) and parts of Poland and Czechoslovakia. After the October (Bolshevik) Revolution these Western countries became independent, until 1939, the year in which a tactical Treaty with Nazi Germany was concluded. Around that time, after a war with Finland, two small parts of the latter country were transferred to the SU and the Baltic states were occupied. At present (1986) the SU consists of fifteen republics, of which the Russian and the Ukrainian Socialist Soviet Republic are by far the largest. The former is subdivided into 49 *oblasti*.

The United States results from the original thirteen British colonies, which declared a war of liberation against England in 1776, which in 1783 (Versailles Peace) finished successfully. The thirteen states established the Union, a confederation, in 1789. Later, the Union was enlarged by former French and Spanish colonies. In the southern states slavery existed, which was not adhered to in the North. Eleven southern states seceded from the Union, which led to the Civil War (1861–65), won by the northern army. In 1865 slavery was abolished. The Constitution was changed—thanks to Presidents Washington and Madison— into a constitution of a federation, and under this constitution a civil war has since become impossible. In 1898 a war with Spain ended with a transfer of Cuba, Puerto Rico and the Philippines to the United States imperium. Cuba and the Philippines were later given their political independence, but, as in so many cases, economic dependence remained.

At present the US is composed of fifty states, and the District of Columbia, around the country's capital, Washington.

12.3   EXAMPLES OF COMPLETED INTEGRATION: MIDDLE-SIZED EUROPEAN NATIONS

In the present section we propose to discuss briefly the integration process through which four middle-sized European countries were shaped.

Germany (D) consisted of more than thirty small and some larger (Prussia, Bavaria) sovereign areas for a long period. In 1871, after the Franco-Prussian war of 1870–1, the nation was unified. On the western side Elsass-Lothringen (Alsace-Lorraine) was part of the 'Reich'; on the eastern side, East Prussia with Danzig and Königsberg, belonged to its territory. Much later than Britain and France, Germany tried to build a colonial empire (mainly in Africa), but lost this after World War I. In 1914 the war started that we now call World War I, and this war was lost by Germany and Austria-Hungary. Alsace-Lorraine returned to France and Poland became an independent country, separating part of East Prussia from the main territory with Danzig (Gdansk) a free city.

World War II (1939–1945) was again lost by Germany and the latter was divided into the Federal Republic of Germany (FRG) and the German Democratic Republic (GDR). The former became a member of the NATO and the European Community (EC), the latter of the WP and the CMEA. The FRG consists of ten *Länder* and West Berlin and is relatively decentralised. The GDR consists of 15 *Bezirke*, including East Berlin, and is relatively centralised.

France was a nation by the seventeenth century: much earlier than Germany and Italy. It had a highly centralised government, which only after World War II introduced some decentralisation by locating parts of the government apparatus outside Paris and by shifting some decision-making to the 22 regions. Education in particular is more centralised than, for instance, German education after World War II. France consists of 92 *départements* whose tasks are limited.

Great Britain also became a nation much earlier (1603) than Germany and Italy. In its most powerful era, the nineteenth century, it consisted of England, Wales, Scotland and Ireland. It had colonies in all parts of the world. Before World War I several of these became 'dominions' with almost complete sovereignty (Australia, New Zealand, Canada) and in 1931 the Empire was changed into the Commonwealth.

After World War II India and Pakistan became independent, Pakistan as an independent Moslem state. All former colonies became members of the Commonwealth. The British Commonwealth now constitutes a cultural and political association for mutual consultation, a rather weak form of integration.

Italy is composed of territories of which some formerly belonged to France, Austria and the Vatican. An attempt to unify all Italian regions in 1848 did not succeed. In 1860 the Sardinian Prime Minister Cavour succeeded in establishing the Kingdom of Italy, to which in 1866 Venice and in 1870 Rome were added. At present Italy is a republic, and in the last few decades the role of the regions has been reinforced.

12.4 EXAMPLES OF COMPLETED INTEGRATION: SMALLER EUROPEAN COUNTRIES

Smaller European countries were integrated before the two middle-sized countries, Germany and Italy. This applies to the Scandinavian countries, the Low Countries (Belgium and the

Netherlands), and Switzerland. Each of these once consisted of several smaller units, between which armed conflicts frequently occurred. By and large such internal wars have not occurred since 1800; Napoleon may have influenced (as a 'common enemy') this process of small-scale integration. Some examples of the opposite process (secession) did occur. Belgium in 1830 liberated itself from an imposed integration, in 1815, with the 'Northern Netherlands'. And Norway separated itself in 1814 from Denmark and in 1905 from Sweden. A complete disintegration of the Austrian-Hungarian 'double monarchy' into small countries (Austria, Czechoslovakia, Hungary, Poland, Romania and Yugoslavia) was another reaction against the imposed integration of this heterogeneous territory, a product of Habsburg power policy in the past.

In this section a few more details will be discussed of the Low Countries and of Switzerland, the nations of the two authors.

As stated, the Northern Netherlands integrated at an early date, during the Eighty-Years War (1568–1648) of liberation from Spain. The main conflict was of a religious character: Calvinist Protestants vs. Catholic Spain. A secondary role was played by the imposition of a (10 per cent!) tax. The present Dutch provinces (except two mainly Catholic and one only recently reclaimed) integrated by concluding the Utrecht Union in 1648. Much later, after having been occupied by Napoleon and liberated again, Belgium and the Netherlands were integrated 'from above' (1815) and, as stated, Belgium liberated itself in 1830, by the 'Belgian resurrection' as the liberation was called in Holland; in 1839 independent Belgium was recognised. During World War II voluntarily Belgium, the Netherlands and Luxembourg decided to cooperate, under the name Benelux, in a number of instruments of socio-economic policy, anticipating similar cooperation in the European Community (EC).

In 1986 the Netherlands (divided into twelve provinces) and Belgium (divided into nine provinces) are both members of the EC and both have hierarchies with municipalities as the smallest political units. Because of language problems, Belgium has a more complicated structure, which we will not discuss here.

The most typical example of the 'integration process from below' is provided by Switzerland or the Helvetian Confederation (Confoederatio Helvetica, CH). This process started in 1291 when the original cantons (*Urkantone*) Schwyz, Unterwalden (2 half-cantons) and Uri constituted the *Eidgenossenschaft* as an act of liberation from Austrian rule. An important year in the process was 1803 when Aargau, Graubünden (Grischun), Sankt Gallen, Ticino, Thurgau and Vaud joined, introducing at the same time three other languages (Romansch in Grischun, Italian in Ticino and French in Vaud). The process terminated in 1815, when Geneva, Neuchâtel and Valais (Wallis) joined. An important reform in 1874 changed the confederation into a federal state. The 'Confederation' maintained its name. In 1980 the canton of Berne was split into a small francophone canton Jura and the far larger German-speaking part. So at present (1986) Switzerland is a federal state with 23 cantons (of which three consist of two half-cantons). In contrast with Belgium, there is hardly any friction among the various linguistic groups.

12.5 SOME ASIAN EXAMPLES

A large part of Asia has a colonial or semi-colonial past. Full-fledged colonies include India, Indonesia, Indochina and some smaller areas. A status with some colonial features has existed in West Asia (the 'Middle East'), a number of Chinese cities (now part of the independent People's Republic of China) and in Siberia (originally inhabited by non-Russians). Tibet is attached to China. Among the countries which have been independent for a long time Japan managed to develop from a somewhat underdeveloped status around 1930 to become one of the world's leading countries, now exporting more technological knowledge than it imports if that knowledge is measured by the money paid for patents or licences. Japan is governed in a rather centralised way, consisting of 47 prefectures, which in terms of population are about four times as large as the French *départements*.

The largest country is of course China—so large that it has to follow the strictest population policy of the world; in fact the best population policy in its goals, although not necessarily in its means. It was integrated long before most western countries. At present the People's Republic of China is divided into 21 provinces, two directly governed cities and five autonomous areas, among which Inner Mongolia and Tibet.

Both India and Indonesia became large integrated countries under colonial rule; their governments strongly prefer to remain unified. This understandable preference is shared by the overwhelming part of their population. In India only the radical Sikhs, but not the moderate mass Sikh party, prefer separation. India typically is rather decentralised and consists of 21 states and nine union territories. Indonesia is more centralised.

12.6 INTEGRATION IN PROCESS: THE EUROPEAN COMMUNITY

By far the most important integration process at present is the ongoing integration process of Western Europe, the development of the European Community (EC). It is important because the participants are modern industrial states and that the process is 'from below', that is, supported by most of the political parties of the countries involved. Although our treatment will be a summary one, we shall nevertheless discuss more concretely the sort of problems that must be solved.

We start with a brief history. The process started with the creation in 1951 (Paris Treaty) of the European Coal and Steel Community (ECSC) at the initiative of the French Minister Robert Schuman and inspired by the 'father of European integration', Jean Monnet. Six nations—France, the Federal Republic of Germany, Italy and Benelux—established a truly supranational community of the coalmining and steel making and processing industries, a complex of production to be supervised by it. The ECSC has had the competence and the power to regulate production of and investments in this complex, since 1952. An attempt to create a European Defence Community was rejected in 1954 by the French Parliament. In 1957 (Rome Treaty) two other communities, the European Atomic Energy Agency (Euratom) and the European Economic Community were created, dealing with nuclear energy and with a number of economic policy components. These started operations in 1958. In 1965 the ECSC High Authority proposed the amalgamation of the three into one European Community. This became effective in 1967.

Membership was extended to the United Kingdom, Denmark and Ireland in 1973 to Greece in 1981 and to Portugal and Spain in 1986.

Some of the most important institutions of the EC are the Commission and its administration, the Council of Ministers and the European Parliament. So far, and hopefully temporarily only, the Council of Ministers is the decision-making agency, but it is not supranational. The Commission, which is supranational, submits proposals to the Council and hence is the more creative organ. The Parliament has existed since 1958, but was elected directly only from 1978. At present (1986) the total number of seats is 518, divided over the member nations as follows: West Germany, France, Italy and the United Kingdom 81, Spain 60,

Netherlands 25, Belgium, Greece and Portugal 24, Denmark 16, Ireland 15 and Luxembourg 6 seats.

Within the Administration some important institutions operate: the European Investment Bank (EIB) and the European Development Fund (EDF) since 1958 (Rome Treaty); in 1960 the European Social Fund (ESF), in 1973 the European Monetary Fund (EMF) and in 1975 the European Regional Fund (ERF) were added.

Among the important political decisions are those about the Common External Tariff (1960), the Common Agricultural Policy (1962), and the Own Financial Means (1970, effective 1975). These consist, in 1986, of the import duties levied at the common outer frontiers and 1.4 per cent of the value added tax revenue of member states.

A particularly important common policy is the development cooperation with the former colonies, extended to 65 countries in 1985, known as the African, Caribbean and Pacific (ACP) countries. They have 15 per cent of the Third World population. The cooperation forms are discussed in joint meetings of the ACP and EC member countries. The amounts of financial assistance and the conditions have been laid down in successive Agreements, concluded in Yaoundé (I, 1964; II, 1969) and Lomé (I, 1975; II, 1979; III, 1984). The amount made available under the Lomé II Treaty amounted to 40 million European Currency Units (ECU), whose value is close to one US dollar.

The European integration process will take considerable additional time and require far more effort. In order to develop into a full Union (as envisaged by the leading politicians involved) a large number of decisions by the Council of Ministers will have to be taken. This does not only apply to the implementation of the Rome Treaty, but even more to the creation of an 'optimal Union' satisfying all conditions of an optimal social order as discussed in Part I of this book. The Rome Treaty's common transportation policy, for instance, has been implemented only very provisionally. The agricultural policy, now taking the larger part of the Community's budget, must be reformed, since it is much too protective and has led to huge surplus stocks. Examples of proposed alternatives are those by Friedeberg (1985) and by Van Riemsdijk (1985); for the purpose of the present book it would lead us too far afield to discuss these and other alternatives.

An example of the hundreds of partial decisions to be made in order to eliminate imperfect competition is the harmonisation of large numbers of technical standards: of biological conditions, quality standards for all sorts of raw materials and industrial products, and so on. Unification of industrial property criteria (patents, trade marks, etc.) is another example.

Industrialists have become active in pointing out the need for one industrial policy for the EC, if it is to become competitive with the US and Japan (cf. Wagner, 1985).

Subjects on which the Rome Treaty is not clear enough are those of the harmonisation of monetary and financial policy. If the EC wants to act as an economic union, the creation of money must be under joint control of the central banks, as the Federal Reserve system in the US. Since the desirable amounts of money creation depend also on the surpluses or the deficits of public budgets, or rather accounts, these must also be determined by a Community decision. Reports such as the Werner Report (1970) and the elaboration of it (Werner, 1977, for instance) analyse these problems, but the corresponding decision-making structure does not (yet) exist. (Cf. also Pinder, 1984.)

Unfortunately the cooperation of some national governments or political parties left much to be desired. President de Gaulle of France did not adhere to the basic idea of integration and his attitude considerably retarded the process. National interests were often seen myopically. Large public enterprises such as railways or telecommunication corporations ordered their capital goods from national manufacturers irrespective of quality and price, as a short-term support for their national employment policy. Similar forms of myopia were shown by socialist parties and trade unions, to the detriment of their own long-term interests.

A macro-economic indication that European integration probably is far below the optimal level can be seen in the fact that in the US the level of federal expenditures (excluding military expenditures) is more than ten times the amount of the EC budget, whereas, by coincidence, the total incomes of US and EC are roughly equal ($2500 billion ($10^9$)). This, then, means that *considerably more elements of national sovereignty have to be shifted to the level of EC.*

12.7   INTEGRATION IN PROCESS ELSEWHERE

Partly in reply to Western European integration in various other parts of the world similar attempts at integration have been made. The most successful attempt no doubt is that of the Andean

Market, including originally Bolivia, Colombia, Ecuador, Peru and Venezuela. Serious attempts were made to agree on some division of labour between the less developed member nations, Colombia and Ecuador and the others. Many of the difficulties experienced in European integration also showed up here. Alongside this most advanced attempt at integration a more general, but less intensive form of integration is in preparation for Latin America as a whole.

A good start has been made in the Caribbean area with the signing of the Treaty of Chaguaramas in 1973. This established the Caribbean Community and Common Market (CARICOM) with 13 members. Its main objectives are to establish a common market, the coordination of foreign policies of member states, and functional cooperation including certain common services (a shipping line, an airline, and education and health services).

In Africa various groupings of countries exist which share some form of cooperation, but hardly provide us with precise directions for world-wide integration. Extreme drought in some parts of Africa and acute political problems require so much attention that more constructive and cautious policies of integration do not get the necessary attention. Some oil-exporting countries, (members of the Organisation of Petroleum Exporting Countries (OPEC)) gave most of their attention to the latter's policies of market regulation.

This also applies to a number of Asian countries, mostly in Western Asia, but also in Indonesia. Attempts at cooperation were thwarted by religious-political controversies such as the Iraq-Iran war and the difficulties surrounding Lebanon and Israel. In Asia, moreover, three large countries (China, India and Indonesia) as a matter of course are less interested in integration; moreover, China is a communist state. The six-member Association of South-East Asian Nations (ASEAN) is a political rather than an econonic association. Its cooperation with Japan may lead to some form of division of labour, but its main economic importance is the North–South character of such a cooperation (cf. Okita, 1980).

Quite recently regional cooperation in South Asia has been taken up again, as stated in the UN publication *Development Forum* (March 1986, p. 12).

12.8 GROUPS OF COUNTRIES IN NEED OF INTEGRATION

There is a wide divergence between the need for integration and political interest in such cooperation. By the need for integration we mean the potential increase in welfare (or at least, well-being) by the creation of larger markets and the ensuing division of labour. This need for integration is largest for groups of small countries. The clearest example are the Caribbean group of countries (cf. section 8.5) and Central America, neighbouring the Caribbean. It is ironic that exactly in that region the propensity to sovereignty is stronger than anywhere in the world. It is here that we find independent nations of less than 100,000 inhabitants; it is here that the island of Aruba, one of the 'Netherlands' Antilles' wants to separate itself from the other $4\frac{1}{2}$. Such a political preference (of its leadership, or of all citizens?) is an expensive hobby. It must be hoped that one day this will be understood.

In the hope that in years to come more reasonable ideas will be expressed we venture to mention one aspect of political strategy that will occur. Where should the process of integration start? In principle, we think, the start should be made by the smallest two. They are the weakest, in all probability, and may gain most from cooperation. The two largest, being the strongest, are likely to gain relatively less. It is conceivable that as a consequence of the soil type, two islands will have the same most competitive product, and consequently, exceptions to our suggestions exist. Complementarity of main product may also be a factor favourable to starting cooperation.

As already mentioned, a good beginning has been made by the Caribbean Community and Common Market (CARICOM) mentioned in the previous section. For more details cf. the interview given by its Secretary General, R. Rainford to *The Courier* (1986). Similarly, also five Central American countries have concluded a General Treaty for Central American economic integration. We hope that the treaty's implementation will be successful.

12.9 HOW TO PREPARE FOR WORLD INTEGRATION

From the historical experience of several industrialised and a few developing countries it appears that integration is one of the most powerful means to end war between the integrated political units (cf. sections 12.2 to 12.5 inclusive). The question makes sense, therefore, whether the process of integration can be advanced. The ultimate aim should be world integration which coincides with what we dealt with as the aim of strengthening the United Nations (cf. Chapter 11). As in other examples discussed (cf. section 12.8), alternative starting points are conceivable. It seems useful to recall a well-known historical lesson, namely that cooperation between independent nations is often facilitated by the existence of a common danger. Some would even maintain that the existence of a common enemy is a precondition to international cooperation. Western European cooperation certainly was furthered by the fear of the SU, as stated by P.-H. Spaak.

Even so, there remain alternative starting points for a further world integration. One possible start is the attempt to construct the building blocks of the world community discussed in sections 5.4 and 11.2. The incentive to start such negotiations might be a decision by the UNGA, on the basis of a report by an independent commission on strengthening the United Nations. We are aware of the ambitious nature of this train of thought. We derive the inspiration to formulate such an ambitious suggestion from the French dictum that great evils can only be treated with the aid of great remedies: *aux grands maux les grands remèdes*. The common danger to each group of nations envisaged as a potential building block would be their loss of any influence on UN decision-making.

Another possible start would be to address the two superpowers. Essentially it is their integration that is the crucial condition for an end to war. Integration, for the time being, can at best mean adherence to one or several treaties on test bans, a ban of weapons in space, a balanced reduction of forces, and so on, but considerably more radical than the treaties adhered to so far. The question is whether the two superpowers can be persuaded that they are threatened by a common danger. The undesirable common danger is the outbreak of war, especially but not exclusively nuclear war. A conventional war could be a danger too. Another common danger is a permanently high military budget.

There might be some other common dangers. The rest of the world might draw some conclusions from Alva Myrdal's statement (1976) that US and SU are playing a game with the rest of us.

These conclusions might be in the field of trade policies, where Japan and Western Europe should play the leading role.

REFERENCES

Europese Almanak (European Almanac) (1976), Brussels, EC.

Friedeberg, A.S. (1985), *How to Reduce Milk Surpluses and Save Taxpayers' Money as well*, Rotterdam, Unilever, N.V.

Myrdal, A. (1976), *The Game of Disarmament. How the United States and Russia Run the Arms Race*, New York, Pantheon Books.

Okita, S. (1980), *The Developing Economies and Japan. Lessons in growth*, Tokyo, University of Tokyo Press.

Pinder, J. (1984), 'Economic Union and the Draft Treaty', *The Federalist* XXVI, 181–98.

Rainford, R. (1986), Interview by *The Courier*, March–April, pp. 2–5.

Scharpf, F.W. (1985), *Die Politikverflechtungsfalle: oder was ist generalisierbar an den Problemen des deutschen Föderalismus und der europäischen Integration?* (The trap of policy intertwining: or which of the problems of German federalism and European integration can be generalised?), Wissenschaftszentrum Berlin, Oktober (Science Centre Berlin, October).

Van Riemsdijk, J.F. (1985), 'Hervorming van het landbouwbeleid van de EG', (Reform of the agricultural policy of the EC), *Econ.-Stat. Berichten* 70, pp. 875–81.

Wagner, G.A. (1985), 'Internationaal recht ontwikkelt zich te traag' (International law develops too slowly), *Onderneming*, 13 December, p. 15.

Werner, P. (1970), *Report to the Council and the Commission on the Stepwise Implementation of the Economic and Monetary Union in the EC* (the Werner Report), Brussels, EC, Supplement to Bulletin 11.

Werner, P. (1977), *L'Europe monétaire reconsidérée* (Monetary Europe reconsidered), Lausanne, Centre de recherches européennes.

13 Towards Peaceful Coexistence

13.1 INTRODUCTION: PURPOSE OF THIS CHAPTER; TRADITIONAL CAUSES OF WAR

In this concluding chapter we shall summarise the results of our analysis of what we feel to be the most important problems of today's world: the organisation of *peace*, a higher *welfare level* and a much *less unequal welfare distribution*. Although the problems are interconnected, we shall consider their main aspects in succession.

The threats to peace have two main origins: the wish of nations to enhance their power, and the wish of some nations to defend or to spread their type of social order. The former may be called the traditional cause of wars and the latter the ideological cause of wars. The traditional cause of war is founded on nationalism and the corresponding preference for sovereignty. These factors also operate in countries whose social philosophy is internationalist, as may be illustrated by the name given by SU leaders to World War II: they call it 'the great patriotic war'.

Our point of view on traditional wars is that nationalism, although understandable, has irrational foundations and the preference for sovereignty rests on a misunderstanding. Nationalism rests on the assumption that the citizens of one's own nation are, essentially, better than those of other nations. This can never be true for all nations involved in a conflict and so must contain irrational elements. The preference for sovereignty rests on the assumption that sovereignty means control of the country's welfare, which is not correct. A sovereign country's welfare is also dependent on what other countries do.

3.2   IDEOLOGICAL CAUSES OF WAR

The ideological causes of war and of today's armament race of the two most powerful blocs (NATO and WP) or the two superpowers are based on the polarising discussions between the proponents of two extreme social orders: *laissez-faire* and central planning. The systems are based on Adam Smith's *Wealth of Nations* and Karl Marx's *Capital*. These books are used almost as bibles and claim to be scientific foundations of the systems; at least, extremists of both factions think that way. The two books appeared, respectively, in 1776 and before or around 1883—the year of Marx's death (and, coincidentally, the year in which Keynes and Schumpeter were born). The authors did not know two fundamental changes in production technologies that would occur later: nuclear energy discovered by Albert Einstein (who in 1883 was four years old) and micro-electronics, a complex of technologies based on the use of digital arithmetics, semi-conductors and miniaturising of the necessary integrated circuits. This combination enabled their users to make feasible and extremely cheap the process of very complicated computing and, with its aid, numerically controlled tools and other capital goods. Both inventions have brought about a revolutionary change in productive forces (*Produktivkräfte*) for civilian as well as military production. The consequences of these revolutionary changes in productive technologies are very important.

13.3   NECESSARY ADAPTATION OF SOCIETAL THEORIES

Because of the important role played by 'productive forces' in both Smithian and Marxian theory, these theories have to be revised or adapted and so have the political strategies based on them: 'capitalist' and 'socialist' strategies. This cannot be done with the aid of the original 'bibles', but has to be done by ourselves, that is, on the basis of knowledge of the new technologies. In Secretary-General Gorbachev's words: 'we are living in a period of accelerated thinking' (Gorbachev, 1986). In some respects the strategy will be different from previous formulations, of Marxism-Leninism (for the communists) or different from previous formulations of economic and security strategies of western political leaders.

This book is an attempt to present such a revision.

Nuclear energy first of all necessitates a revision of military thinking. A nuclear war using the currently available quantities of nuclear energy (which are about a million times those available in 1945 and used to bomb Hiroshima and Nagasaki) is a war without victors. A nuclear attack means suicide. This is so different from conventional military thinking that considerable areas of such military thinking have become baseless. Annihilation means that the use of nuclear armament as a threat loses its credibility and the consequences of this revised theory have not yet been drawn; let alone, penetrated into the military theories adhered to.

13.4   OFFENSIVE AND DEFENSIVE WEAPONS

It is ironical—or rather, tragic—that the development of armament by the two superpowers after 1945 was copied from Hitler, the agressor-in-principle by developing his rockets, which are essentially *offensive* weapons. Had the military and the politicians known what is now known, they might have searched from the start for new *defensive* weapons. Now that both the SU and the US are overarmed with offensive weapons, any attempt to search autonomously for defensive weapons against rockets is extremely destabilising to the military balance, because the partner who first discovers such a defensive weapon obtains first-strike capability. The only safe way to switch from offensive to defensive weapons is a common search, a search for common security, as set out by the Palme Commission (Palme *et al.*, 1982 and 1985). Moreover, as long as mutual distrust continues it is doubtful what common search means; and the only way might be a common non-search, that is a ban on certain types of armament.

The shift to defensive weapons is essential because the only absolute certainty about a nation's non-offensive intentions can be obtained by the country's inability to be offensive, i.e. not to have offensive weapons. And it can only permit itself to do away with its offensive if it has built up an equivalent defensive capacity. In the long run there is a choice between the ban on a number of weapon types and the building up of defensive armament; in the short run a ban seems to be the only possibility, provided verification is accepted.

13.5   CHOICE OF SOCIAL ORDER POSSIBLE ONLY IN FRAMEWORK OF SECURITY

The choice of a preferred social order is an area in which each country should be sovereign. Within the limits set by the SU this was adhered to by the CMEA in the Berlin 1976 meeting. In that meeting each member nation was given the right to choose 'its own way to socialism'. The limits set by the SU can be observed from the WP intervention in Czechoslovakia in 1968 and in Hungary in 1956. The relative freedom can be judged from the deviations between Kádár's Hungarian and other régimes. Recently somewhat more freedom seems to have been recognised.

In the western world and in the Third World this sovereign right is recognised within wider limits. Even so a tendency exists for the superpowers to set certain limits, as in Nicaragua by the US. This implies the possibility that one of the superpowers will intervene if a country chooses a social system rejected by that superpower. Such intervention can only be avoided if a system of world security exists, excluding military interference by any country, and the International Court of Justice decides on the legitimacy of a national choice.

A clear divergence exists between the rhetorics of social system choice and reality. Propaganda is made on both sides for the extreme orders: *laissez-faire* and central planning. These extremes are the only social orders which do not exist! All existing social orders are mixed: the US has a limited degree of social security, and the SU has limited private property of means of production: land plots and private service firms (cf. Adler Karlsson, 1967).

This state of affairs should be recognised more openly and help to enhance the degree of cooperation between the world's nations, particularly between the superpowers. This is a fundamental change in strategy needed because of the lethality of nuclear weaponry; it means a choice for tolerance instead of polarisation. This is a democratic socialist and at the same time a Western European message!

13.6   THE NEED FOR PEACEFUL CHANGE AND PEACEFUL COEXISTENCE

In a world order without war the possibility of changing that order must not be excluded. If change were not possible existing inequities would be doomed to stay. Changing the world order must remain possible. In the past such changes were often brought about by violence; if we want to exclude violence, an alternative means must exist. This is a task of the International Court of Justice. In order for the Court to be able to pass judgements it cannot only rely on existing law. New international law will have to be created; one important source is the opinions of experts on economic and security orders. This is one of the justifications for the integration of socio-economic and security policies as attempted in this book. As a matter of course other integration processes are highly desirable—for instance, the integration of the aspects just mentioned with cultural and religious aspects (cf. section 8.4). Here too the role of tolerance must be stressed. In history intolerant religious attitudes repeatedly have done enormous harm to human welfare. There is considerable similarity between religious beliefs and extreme political attitudes; we have already mentioned the role of the 'bibles' of the extremist proponents of *laissez-faire* or communism.

If peaceful coexistence is what we want—and we do urgently need it—a spirit of tolerance is needed. American leadership must learn to live in a world where communists live; and the Russian leadership must learn to live in a world where private initiative is adored! Not only must they learn this: they may even have to teach it. In well-known Marxian language: a revaluation of all values (*eine Umwertung aller Werte*).

13.7   FOUNDATIONS OF OUR THINKING ABOUT AN OPTIMAL WORLD ORDER

Our thinking about an optimal world order must be inspired by (i) *managerial thinking*, and (ii) the *existing structure* of *efficiently-run countries*. In a hierarchy we can learn from what operates successfully at a lower level in that same hierarchy. In both cases the theory of the optimum level of decision-making for the solution of a given problem can be the principle to start from (cf. Scharpf, 1985).

The present structure of the United Nations needs fundamental changes based on the sources of inspiration mentioned. Important countries, in terms of population size and income per capita, need to have more voting power than less important countries. This does not need to go as far as in the IMF or the WBG, but certainly clearly into that direction. In IMF and WBG the influence of population size should be reinforced, parallel to the development in the parliaments of the oldest democracies. Research is needed to make more precise choices. Research is also needed on whether the world should be divided up into 12 to 15 blocks to be represented in the decision-making body—an *intermediate level* between the executive power and the majority of member countries. Most small member countries could be represented in one of the blocks; some very large countries could be blocks in their own right. The research recommended could draw on the experience and from the errors of the European Community. The degree of integration, for instance, of the EC is much to low, as a comparison with the US shows (cf. section 12.6, final paragraph).

13.8 FIRST STEPS TOWARDS PEACEFUL COOPERATION: SOCIO-ECONOMIC

The preceding sections deal with the long-term and mid-term reforms recommended and will meet with scepticism of many 'short-term politicians'. In the two final sections we now summarise what in the short term can be steps in the direction advocated. As in Chapters 8 and 9 we will use current jargon and summarise what must be done to help solve the North–South problem and the East–West problem; in other words, the socio-economic problem of income inequality between developed and developing countries and the security problem of overarmament of the superpowers (and their allies). This section deals with the North–South problems and their solution, and on many points subscribes to the Brandt Commission recommendations (Brandt, 1980 and 1983). Important recommendations are the expansion of the money circulation (the IMF's Special Drawing Rights should have been doubled instead of having been increased by 47 per cent); and not have imposed deflation to so many countries. Imports of industrial products should not have been subject to quotas and the Multifibre Agreement discontinued. Financial transfers to developing countries must be increased and debts rescheduled and partly be remitted. Commodity agreements should be concluded for more products, including sugar and cocoa. Technology introduced by transnational enterprises should be adapted to the relative scarcity of factors of production and the optimal lot size and physical characteristics of products. A larger role of self-reliance of developing countries is desirable and programmes of cooperation should correspond to the special circumstances in the various continents. The least developed countries—especially in Africa—require a directed agriculture strategy.

13.9 FIRST STEPS TOWARDS PEACEFUL COOPERATION: SECURITY ISSUES

The transfer of sovereignty needed to enhance security can be started by the continued adherence to treaties concluded in the past and the conclusion of new treaties discussed in recent years. Ideas expressed by the Palme Commission and by the leadership of the superpowers in and after the Geneva summit in November 1985 and the Reykjavik discussion on 11 and 12 October 1986 deserve implementation.

Thus, continued adherence to the Non-Proliferation Treaty (1967), the Anti-Ballistic Missile Treaty (1972) and the Strategic Arms Limitation Treaty II (1979) and signing of the NPT by all non-nuclear states should be a start; followed by the conclusion of a Comprehensive Test Ban Treaty, a ban on weapons in space, a further negotiation of the SU proposal on peaceful cooperation in space, a ban on chemical weapons, a ban on anti-satellite arms and the creation of a nuclear-free zone in Central Europe.

The change in leadership in the SU was followed by new proposals on both sides. A comprehensive programme of disarmament was proposed by Secretary-General Gorbachev on 15 January 1986. The portion dealing with intermediate-range missiles was not linked to any conditions regarding the SDI and might be a first item for continued negotiations. But short-term negotiations cannot be the subject of a book like the present one. So we must leave that to other means of communication.

The role to be played by well-ordered negotiations will be extremely important for the world's future. This may have contributed to the choice of a new project by the International Institute for Applied Systems Analysis (IIASA) in Laxenburg, Austria, on Processes of International Negotiation (PIN). Among the negotiation processes that have been complicated and successful those used to attain consensus about the new Law of the Sea deserve particular attention (cf. section 11.5).

In the past, when governments have made a deliberate decision to seek improved relations, it has often been possible to overcome old hostilities very rapidly, and the same can and must happen again. For example, when the US and Chinese governments took the first small steps to improve relations, attitudes in the two countries changed from great mutual suspicion to curiosity and even friendship within a few years. As late as 1969, during the US debate whether or not to build an anti-ballistic missile (ABM) system, the argument was put forward that it was not yet technically feasible to build a 'dense' ABM system against SU missiles, but that was not so important, since the Soviet leaders were relatively reasonable and reliable. The greatest danger were the Chinese: they were so 'fanatic and unpredictable', it was said. Most important was to build at least a 'thin' ABM system as a protection against Chinese nuclear missiles. Today, the US is no longer afraid of a Chinese nuclear attack, but not because of any 'thin' ABM system. It is because the US and China have normalised their relations. Over 17,000 Chinese students are studying in the US, and many Americans visit China each year. There is growing trade between those two countries. This is what has brought greater security to them and less mutual fear, not a purely technical solution. There is no reason why a similar improvement in US–SU relations could not also occur, if the will is present on both sides.

The old idea that it is possible to gain unilateral security at the expense of other countries' security has become obsolete in the nuclear age. If others perceive us to be a threat to their security, so much that they wish we would disappear from the face of the earth, and if they have the means to make us disappear, we cannot be very secure. To be secure we should, on the contrary, see to it that we are so useful—preferably indispensable—to others that they would be very disappointed if we did indeed disappear. In the nuclear age, there can only be common security, or no security for anyone.

NOTE

1. In a conversation on 15 April 1986 between Secretary-General Gorbachev and the Swedish Prime Minister Carlsson.

Index